LAYING THE FOUNDATION

To Catherine

Laying the Foundation

_— another Heritage Building !
Stop him before he lays
some more._

A CENTURY OF HISTORY AT UNIVERSITY OF TORONTO

_Merry Xmas 1991
Bob B_

ROBERT BOTHWELL

Department of History
University of Toronto

Copyright 1991 by the Department of History, University of Toronto
Printed in Canada by the University of Toronto Press

ISBN 0-7727-8875-8

TO ELEANOR AND ALICE BOTHWELL

Canadian Cataloguing in Publication Data

Bothwell, Robert, 1944–
Laying the foundation

Includes bibliographical references.
ISBN 0-7727-8875-8

1. University of Toronto. Dept. of History –
History.   2. History – Study and teaching (Higher) –
Ontario – Toronto – History.   I. University of
Toronto. Dept of History.   II. Title.

D15.5.T67B68 1991   907'.1'1713541   C91-095403-8

Design: William Rueter

Contents

Foreword

ROFESSOR BOTHWELL has demonstrated both courage and consummate skill in writing this history of the University of Toronto's Department of History. Writing the history of a Department of History is a delicate undertaking. The readers will have been trained, perhaps by the author himself, to criticize the narrative and to analyse the narrator. However sympathetic they may be (this is, after all, their own history), they have learned to question and demur. With such an audience in mind, Professor Bothwell has written a carefully crafted and stimulating history.

We alumni and staff of the department are the beneficiaries. Some readers will have lived more than half of the history described herein, but most of us enter into the story only briefly, or late in the day. For all, reading this history will be an engaging experience. By recalling the broad outlines of the story, Professor Bothwell encourages us to place our own experiences in the larger historical context. He reminds us of much that we had forgotten, and shows us much that we never knew. If our interpretations of events should differ, or our perspective vary from his, we owe to him this chance to clarify and to formulate our stand.

As we begin the second century of history at Toronto, it is important to reflect on the ways that the department has shaped us just as we have shaped it. Bothwell's book reminds us that the department is neither unchanging nor is it remade with each generation. We all carry with us the weight of the department's past, a weight that is sometimes a burden to be shrugged off, and sometimes a source of stability and identity to be fostered. As we shape a department to meet the opportunities and challenges of the twenty-first century, we can look forward to the year 2091, when someone will continue the story that Professor Bothwell has begun so well.

Joe Goering
Acting Chair, Department of History
University of Toronto

Acknowledgments

THIS BOOK had its origins in an impromptu conversation in 1988 with Michael Finlayson, then the chairman of the Department of History. In suggesting that I write the history of the department, Michael promised his full support, and throughout this project he was both encouraging and supportive.

My research assistants, Francine McKenzie and Luis Sarabia, were invaluable and indefatigable. The results of their industry and intelligence are apparent on every page; of course, any errors and omissions are mine alone. Alex Reford also provided helpful informa-tion. Harold Averill and the other staff members of the University of Toronto Archives furnished informed advice and helped out in every conceivable way. Robin Harris's pioneering work in assembling materials for the history of the university eased my task.

Ian Drummond, the historian of the now defunct Department of Political Economy, gave me the benefit of his learning, experience, and wise advice. So did John Cairns, Ken McNaught, Paul Rutherford, Craig Brown, Joe Goering, and Ian Radforth, all of whom read the manuscript and gave timely warnings of error. Vicki Dingillo and Gail Murray also read the manuscript and managed its transition from a collection of bytes to a finished disc. Philip Creighton gave unfettered access to his father's papers at the National Archives of Canada. Thayron Sandquist, Joe Goering, and Doug Owram also made very useful suggestions. Fred Thorpe, my old superior at the National Museum of Canada, and Margaret Banks of the University of Western Ontario made a very special effort, for which this book is, I believe, much the better. To those who patiently endured interviews or sent in suggestions or a record of their experiences at the University of Toronto, I am profoundly grateful. My old friend and long-term colleague Rosemary Shipton once again shepherded another of my manuscripts past many editorial perils.

And to my daughters Alice and Eleanor I owe particular thanks for putting up with yet one more book and its consequences. Their good humour through the writing of this history more than anything else made its completion possible.

LAYING THE FOUNDATION

CHAPTER ONE

By Way of Prologue

Visitors approaching the University of Toronto often find themselves well within its boundaries before noticing a change in their surroundings. The people change first, from the shoppers or provincial civil servants to the east and north of the campus to throngs of hurrying students and the occasional harassed professor. The buildings change next, from shabby on the outskirts of the campus, where the university owns but does not occupy, to the various forms of monumental styles favoured in successive generations since the university was effectively established in 1853. (It was actually founded a generation before, in 1827, but for twenty-five years it remained an endowment in search of a function.) Some of the older buildings sit around parklands and playing fields. Others, more recent if not more modern, line one of Toronto's arterial roads, St George Street, in the brick and concrete boxlike shapes popular among the architects of the 1950s and 1960s. Their windswept plazas are deserted, except for seagulls and other scavengers, for half the year – the teaching half – especially around the home of the Faculty of Arts and Sciences, Sidney Smith Hall. Finally, on closer inspection, the monuments turn shabby again, mute testimony to government's funding abilities and policies. At that point the visitor has arrived.

St George Street is an apt place to start a tour of the campus. The original St George was a French royalist refugee of the 1790s, who took the name of Britain's patron saint in gratitude for his escape from the guillotine. St George afterwards became a successful merchant in the town of York, capital of the British frontier province of Upper Canada. He returned to Paris in 1815 with the end of the Napoleonic wars, leaving behind his name to puzzle future eras.

Sidney Smith Hall, at 100 St George Street, has a name more recently derived: that of the president of the University of Toronto from 1945 to 1957. After Sidney Smith's untimely death in 1959 – the consequence of leaving academe for federal politics, some said – the university named its newest and most modern construction, a hall for the social sciences, in his honour. When the building opened in 1961, a gaggle of departments was moved there, from fine arts, on top, to psychology, in the basement. Drifting in between, on the second, third, and fifth floors, was the Department of History, which has dwelt there ever since.

Universities are prone to commemorations. Across St George Street is a yellow brick, Georgian-style building. The property of University College, it was designed as its men's residence and appropriately named after Sir Daniel Wilson, president of the college in the 1880s and first professor of English and history at the university in 1853. Wilson almost predated the university, and certainly predated the Department of History; only part of his duties related to the teaching of this subject. Wilson is also the only historian whose name can be found on the mute honour roll of buildings scattered around the campus.

There is a curious symbolism in "history's" lack of embodiment in the university's visible history. Retrospective nomenclature is effectively a triumph of form over substance. There is also a balance of fortune. Abused and unappreciated by their teaching staff during their administrative lifetimes, university presidents doubtless need some recompense, some recognition that will be at least neutral. Petrifaction in a cornerstone is, in this sense, both just and harmless. History's monument must be elsewhere.

History was present at the university's foundation, and when the history of the university as a whole comes to be written the teaching of history will doubtless prove to be an important part. Historians at the university and students of history have played significant roles in the life of Toronto, Ontario, and Canada. What they wrote, and what they taught, influenced the development of their country and helped shape Canadians' approach to a wider world. As professionals, historians at the University of Toronto have participated in the development of their profession and in the life of the mind in Canada and abroad.

The locus of their work has been the Department of History at the University of Toronto. "The Department" is, of course, *one* department among many at the university. It is in some senses a corporate fiction, a collective illusion that serves to mask over time the individual activities of hundreds of professors and thousands of students. But what shrouds also sustains. The function of any academic department is to organize the presentation of knowledge to students, but it also institutionalizes relations and relationships among its members – undergraduate, graduate, and professional. As such, it is a factor in the life of many minds, and in many lives.

But only a factor. This is an institutional history, not a collective biography or an investigation of the function of history in the Canadian psyche. It is an analysis of relationships in a given place, the University of Toronto, in a limited time: a hundred years overall, three or four years for most, forty years for some. The "History of History" cannot claim to be intellectual history, though it may contribute to it by describing the circumstances in which intellects functioned. It is not simply professional history, the development of a small group of professors into a larger group of professors, though it is partly that.

Nor is it "student" history or "youth" history, in which historians over thirty seek to plumb the background of those beneath them in age and beyond them in time and experience. But it is partly that too.

In form it is a narrative, a story, and, like any good story, it begins at a beginning, though not necessarily at the beginning.

Ontario had a history before it had historians. There was the history of indigenous aboriginal groups – the Huron, the Neutral, the Petun, and the Ojibwa. There was the history of invading nations – the French, the Iroquois, and the British. There was the history of refugees – Iroquois again and British Americans, the United Empire Loyalists. Finally, there was the history of immigrants, brought over from the British Isles in separate waves to the fertile peninsula of Upper Canada, whose soil in short order yielded prosperity, income, and taxes.

The taxes flowed to the provincial capital of York, later Toronto, with its mélange of merchants, manufacturers, and civil servants. It was in York that the province's unique institutions would be concentrated: the legislature, the lieutenant-governor, the bishop (Anglican), and other place-holders. And it was in York that the government proposed to found a provincial university, Anglican in character and loyal in politics, that would perpetuate the values and beliefs of Upper Canada's founders. In 1827 King's College was duly chartered.

Such an institution, from such sponsors, was bound to excite opposition. The provincial university remained practically moribund for decades while Upper Canada's religious and political leaders squabbled about forms of government, the nature of government, and the proper beneficiaries of government. A university building was erected near Taddle Creek, north of the city, and then abandoned to another more urgent purpose – to serve as the provincial lunatic asylum. Too elitist in character and too narrow in its political and religious base (although Anglicans remained the largest denomination in Toronto itself), the province's educational system awaited reform. And reform took time.

It was not until the 1840s, with responsible government and a political party system in place, that the government again turned its attention to higher education. The government by then was that of the Province of Canada – Upper and Lower Canada united, and then divided again, administratively, into Upper and Lower branches. Upper Canada remained emphatically British, not least because of the waves of immigration that washed over the province after 1815; but the province was affected, too, by its environment, and its environment was overwhelmingly American. The Americans had resolved their own problems of church and state by separating the two, abolishing state churches and removing the preference given to the Anglican or Congregational churches. And so, decades later, it was done in Upper Canada.

Upper Canadian reformers had long cherished the idea of abolishing the Anglican privilege of King's College. Robert Baldwin, the Upper Canadian reform leader, almost got secularization passed in 1843, only to be derailed. When, finally, a reform government came to power in the Province of Canada in 1848, the university question was one of its first preoccupations.[1] On 31 December 1849 Anglican King's College became the secular University of Toronto. Not quite four years later, in 1853, the university was again reorganized by Baldwin's successor, Francis Hincks, and a teaching arm, University College, established within the university. Provision was made for religious foundations to affiliate or, as the term went, to "federate" with the provincial institution, an idea interpreted by the secular Globe newspaper as a sectarian grab for the provincial university's endowment.[2] A complicated administrative structure was created for the university, with a chancellor, a vice-chancellor, and a president; and a senate and a board of trustees to boot. In the spirit of the times all these high offices were placed directly under the provincial government – that is, under the politicians and the provincial cabinet. The Senate undertook the task of defining the university: what would be taught, and how, and how much.

It was the provincial cabinet that had to find funds for the provincial university, and the advantage of such funding as far as the politicians were concerned was by no means obvious. The secular principle was not universally popular. One after another the province's religious denominations struck out on their own to establish colleges for the training of their flocks: the Methodists already had one – Victoria College at Cobourg – and the Anglicans, Roman Catholics, and Presbyterians quickly followed suit. Moreover, the University of Toronto proved extravagant in its expenditure, spending what remained of King's College's endowment on the new University College, a couple of hundred yards from the original university building in Queen's Park.

University College would be constructed between 1856 and 1859 in every conceivable style, from Romanesque to neo-Gothic. The governor general, Sir Edmund Head, was an enthusiastic participant in the design and construction of the college, and others contributed their ideas. The professor of history and English literature contributed sketches of gargoyles and designed some of the interior woodwork. Daniel Wilson, LLD, had in his youth laboured for the painter J.M.W. Turner in London before abandoning art as unprofitable; but art still had its uses. A generation raised on romantic novels and tales of medieval derring-do saw nothing odd in that; from its Gothic tower of learning the university could gaze down on the city, in one direction, or onto its cloisters, alive with fee-paying students, in the other. But despite the necessary intrusion of money into the cloister, the university's soaring medievalism symbolized the isolation of the sublime from the sordid and of true scholarship from mundane money-grubbing.

It is with Daniel Wilson that history first appeared on the curriculum of the University of Toronto. A Scotsman ("Scotch" to nineteenth-century Torontonians), born in Edinburgh in 1816 and educated at the city's high school, Wilson's formal university training was brief. A year into his studies, he threw them over to study engraving. Art did not provide a living, Wilson found, but writing did, especially when he could act as his own illustrator. Pot-boilers, both books and essays, flowed from Wilson's pen in London and in Edinburgh until, in 1848, he struck a popular chord with his *Memorials of Edinburgh in the Olden Time*, lavishly illustrated by his own facile hand. The *Memorials* pointed Wilson in the direction of antiquarianism and its first cousin, archaeology; he became Scotland's first archaeologist and contributed the word "prehistory" to the English language. Many sentimental Scots now bought and prized Wilson's works. The readers included one Scot in temporary exile in Quebec City, James Bruce, fourth earl of Elgin.[3]

The fourth earl was governor general of Canada. It was under his auspices that the local politicians were finally given their head and allowed access to the lush fields of self-government and political patronage. At first Elgin found the consequences of reign without rule a risky business, but after 1850 politics were calmer and the governor found it possible to try his hand at the gentler arts of culture and education. The university, it turned out, needed a professor of history.

Where the demand for a historian originated is unclear. History was an accepted part of life and culture. History differentiated Upper Canada from New York State and from Lower Canada. History linked British America to Great Britain. History helped define politics, and other contemporary things as well. History to many Upper Canadians meant little more than the Bible and Foxe's *Book of Martyrs*; nevertheless, Canadian politics in the nineteenth century witnessed the daily application of scripture and Protestant (or Catholic) martyrology to the ordering of daily life, or education, or the country. Those better educated or more fortunate might boast a shelf of Gibbon's *Decline and Fall of the Roman Empire* or, more likely, Sir Walter Scott's immensely popular historical romances. Perhaps every good college had to have someone to teach "history," if only as a means to the better appreciation of literature, though history's standing was hardly universally admitted. In English-speaking universities it lagged after classics, philosophy, and English, with which subjects it was often combined. As late as the 1880s there were no more than twenty history professors in the United States. At Princeton the professor of history taught political science as well, admittedly a closer fit than English literature.[4]

The news of the establishment of a chair of history and English – as soon as a professor could be got – attracted attention. On 22 July 1851 Daniel Wilson of Edinburgh sent in his application for the post, accompanied by eighteen printed testimonials from a variety of intellectual personages as well as four Scottish lords and two medical doctors. That fall, T.J. Robertson, headmaster of the provincial Normal School, was granted permission by the Council of Public Instruction, his governing body, to apply for the job.[5] The university Senate deliberated the matter at length over the summer and fall of 1852, with frequent postponements. The minutes for 18 August of that year note the constitution of three chairs – natural philosophy, modern languages, and history and English literature. On 4 December four names were placed in nomination for the chairs of modern languages and history and English: T.J. Robertson (moved by no less a personage than the Reverend Dr Egerton Ryerson, superintendent of schools for the province and Robertson's boss), the Reverend G. Esson, the Reverend O. Burns, and, finally, Dr Daniel Wilson of Edinburgh.[6] Burns's nomination was rejected, and only three names – Esson, Robertson, and Wilson – went forward. These names were duly forwarded to the provincial government and, through the government, to the governor general.[7]

That Daniel Wilson, an antiquarian and ethnologist, was appointed to the Toronto chair should have occasioned no surprise. There was no professional qualification or particular training that would have prepared him for the task. By the standards of his day, and of the university, he was eminently suitable. He had the appropriate title, Doctor, albeit honorary, from St Andrew's University in recognition of his services to Scottish prehistory. The circumstances, specialization, and professionalization that would make him obsolete lay in the future, though not very far in the future; by a curious twist of fate those circumstances moved to Toronto in Wilson's lifetime.

In academic matters, at least where history was concerned, Europe was different from North America. At Oxford and Cambridge there had been Regius professors of history since the time of George I. The cause of history had not gained thereby. The great British historians of the eighteenth and early nineteenth centuries were amateurs; only after 1850 did Oxford and Cambridge seriously teach history. At Oxford, as in the United States, history was combined with another subject: in this case, law, a linkage that closely reflected the English common-law tradition and a connection that gave the learning and teaching of history a peculiar relevance to the study of the common law.[8]

In Germany, Georg Ranke and his disciples were establishing a new way of writing history and of training historians. These developments were dimly perceived across the Atlantic, with varying results. In the British colonies, Oxford grew in prestige and attractiveness as the century wore on. In the United States, the low costs and high prestige of a German education encouraged a trickle of young Americans to travel to the continent in search of learning.[9] They seldom gave a second glance to northern Britain and its peculiar traditions. It was, however, Edinburgh that Daniel Wilson knew.

That may have been a useful qualification. Politicians and the public wanted a vocational university and a practical education. It was that practical education that Wilson felt himself eminently qualified to provide. The new professor belonged to what was called, not without a certain assertive ostentation, "the Scottish Common Sense School."

This, according to Brian McKillop, harmonized "the design of the mind and a conservative social ethic," the very thing for a practical frontier province and its eminently practical politicians. The secularization of the university had displaced the quest for an other-worldly vocation, but at a price. Wilson in his common-sense way showed how the price of "the practical duties of life" could be paid.[10]

Common sense made it necessary to exclude religious quarrels from the classroom, a truth that Upper Canadians already appreciated after decades of religious bickering. Sectarianism rather than religion was the foe. Wilson believed that secular study made manifest God's design for the world.

In travelling to America, Wilson doubtless hoped he was leaving Scottish sectarianism behind. He hoped, eventually, that he would return triumphant to Edinburgh and take up the task of teaching Scottish undergraduates, but for the moment his energies were directed to this new challenge. As he started out in the summer of 1853, he also brought with him his particular combination of ideology and character: a preference for the system he knew, a healthy contempt for the effete Oxford model, a natural stubbornness, and a combative temper. It was a relief, at least, that he was leaving behind Scottish sectarianism and starting afresh at a secular foundation where one's religion counted not at all for admission or for graduation.

He soon needed all his psychic resources. His first trial was Dr John McCaul, university vice-chancellor and president of University College. Dining with Dr McCaul on 22 September 1853, Wilson discovered that the president very much favoured turning his chair of English and history into a chair of ancient history. Wilson instantly perceived he was confronting "all the old scholastic exclusive preference for everything classical." He firmly told the president that he, Wilson, was the best judge of what he would teach.[11]

It was the first of many hostile encounters: over the years Wilson gained the reputation of being "one of McCaul's most strenuous adversaries."[12]

Fortunately the students impressed Wilson more favourably than the president. The difficulty was, he confided to his diary, that he would have to lead his class through three years of learning, with fresh lectures every year – a burden unknown in Scotland. There were so few books available that he decided to write out every fourth lecture at length, so as to provide his students with examples of good written style. A complaint to Dr McCaul elicited £75 to buy library books in his field, but too late in the season to make any difference to the existing academic year. In the meantime Wilson invited his charges to tea, reasoning they would not think the less of him for it, and he started up a debating society.[13] We do not know precisely what Wilson's students thought of him: to the neighbourhood children this tall, bearded figure was "Daddy Long Legs," a Toronto character who strode oblivious from home to campus, pausing every now and then to argue with friends, "with the wind blowing his long beard in every direction and his clothes flapping around him."[14]

Wilson's secular preferences did not mean that Toronto's new history professor was irreligious or that he believed scholarship was at odds with religion. On the contrary, Wilson expected that scholarship and research would make manifest God's works. He did not believe that the clergy were the best judge of such matters: sectarian intervention in matters of science was at least very likely to muddle God's design and frustrate its revelation. Clerically dominated colleges were therefore by definition a bad thing, bad for scholarship by limiting free inquiry, and bad for society by raising artificial barriers between citizens and by wasting scarce resources that might better have been spent on a university open to all. These views were entirely appropriate, and almost a precondition, for a professor in Upper Canada's newly secular university. Wilson, proceeding from common sense, never wavered in his belief that resources should be spent in only one way and therefore in one place: on the University of Toronto.

The situation was complicated by the fact that the religious were not entirely lacking in resources, economic and political. They had their own colleges, and therefore their own students. It was easy to conceive a policy whereby the door remained open to those religious colleges that wished to federate with the university, and, singly and jointly, the religious colleges cautiously sniffed at the proposition. The price – the abandonment of existing buildings and relocation, in some cases, hundreds of miles away – offended local as well as sectarian sensibilities. At the same time, the provincial government of John Sandfield Macdonald encouraged union by cancelling in 1868 its assistance to Queen's, Victoria, and Regiopolis colleges and concentrating its funds on the provincial university alone.[15]

The results were mixed and decidedly slow in coming, but Wilson was not one to wait. Egerton Ryerson charged that University College provided its students with an education that was at once godless, pointless, and luxurious, and that the teaching of history was superfluous. In the preferred model of Oxford and Cambridge, students concentrated on classics and mathematics, not on a subject like history, which in any case was adequately served in the province's secondary schools.

Wilson was expected to respond, and respond he did. Before a legislative committee in 1860 he testified that Oxford and Cambridge were a poor prototype for the Upper Canadian university, not least because they failed utterly to give the teaching of English and history pride of place. The Scottish universities, particularly Edinburgh, were far superior. Ryerson and Wilson then traded abuse as to their respective qualifications to comment on university curricula (neither had a university degree, and Ryerson had never even attended a university). As for university federation, Wilson thereafter took the darkest possible view: it was a Methodist plot to plunder the public treasury.[16]

The story of Wilson's continuing feud with godly education, fascinating and colourful as it was, lies mainly outside the purview of this book. His 1860 testimony merits attention for another reason. In citing the Scottish model of higher education he was signalling the appearance of a unique aspect of the University of Toronto's educational practice: the division of its educational system into *honours* and *pass* courses.

The simple term "courses" has had a variety of meanings in the University of Toronto context. Originally a "course" was a *course of study*, a prescribed sequence of subjects. Wilson and his colleagues established two methods of qualifying for the BA degree: the "fixed" or "pass" course; and the honours course. These courses evolved over time, and there is little point in rehearsing the detailed curricular changes that occurred.[17] The system was, in any case, so complicated as to be almost unintelligible to outsiders; mastering the system and its confusing and confused terminology would itself almost have qualified a student for a degree.

Essentially the pass course exposed the student to a general but fairly rigid curriculum over four years. Pass students took courses in a variety of subjects, including history in second and third years. Although there was some choice, especially in the third and fourth years, it was impossible for a student to take more than two courses in history or less than one.

Honours courses were different. They depended on departments, "the five which had long been distinguished by the assignment of medals in the final examination," including "Modern Languages with History." Each department was responsible for an honours course, and every course had its particular courses of instruction. These were designed to feed specialized knowledge, in quantity, to the undergraduates. Such a course was, as the university recognized, not to every taste: and so provision was made that those who failed an honours course would revert to the pass course. The emergence of a two-tiered system with a clear hierarchy and priority proved to be one of the most enduring characteristics of the University of Toronto, a feature that distinguished it from almost all other North American universities –

but not from Toronto's Scottish spiritual forebears. It was an indication of where the faculty placed its hopes and its affections – and, not coincidentally, its time and attention.[18]

The term "department" is easy to misconstrue. The university departments of the nineteenth century were tiny affairs whose identity was defined by the course of study they taught. A department might consist of one person, or several. Its responsibilities included teaching and examination, as well as graduation (hence the term "graduating departments"), but lecturers and examiners were not always the same people. Departments were ruled by their respective Professors – with a capital P – who sometimes had funds for more junior appointments within their grasp.[19]

From the student's point of view there were a number of advantages to the University of Toronto's new system. There was choice, up to a point: the choice between honours and pass, and the choice among the various honours courses. That choice, once made, led to a rigidly prescribed and closely supervised curriculum – at least in theory. Intellectually and socially such a structure encouraged a pooling of knowledge and resources among students and created a distinctive sense of identity. It brought students to the attention of their professors through a process of personal selection in which undergraduates in their first year sought admission to the honours course. At the same time, it was clear that the pass (or, as it came to be called, the general) course had less prestige, at least as far as the faculty was concerned.[20]

But while Wilson continued, year in and year out, to teach history, sometimes in conjunction with his defeated rival for the professorship, T.J. Robertson, history was never his principal interest. Indeed, while Wilson established a continuing reputation as a controversialist, archaeologist, and scholar of English literature, he wrote little or nothing on history.[21] At the University of Toronto in Wilson's day, history existed without historians to teach it. And in this, as we have seen, Toronto was not unique.

What, then, did Wilson teach, and to whom? The second question is more easily answered than the first. The university's student clientele broadly reflected Ontario society. Far from acting as an elite school, as hostile critics sometimes charged, the university served a very broad spectrum of Ontario society including, after 1884, women, at the insistence of the Liberal provincial government.

What was taught varied considerably over time – and Wilson taught for thirty-nine years. Wilson's students took history and English. The two subjects were examined together, presumably on the basis of Wilson's lectures and whatever reading his students had been able to scrounge at the college library. The coursework that emerges was broadly progressive in form and chronological in organization. In 1855, for example, pass students in the first year were asked to "name the reputed founders of the Egyptian, Assyrian and Babylonian monarchies" and to "Give the dates of the first and second invasions of Britain by Julius Caesar," among other subjects. The second year was more advanced, chronologically: "What event in European history marks the commencement of the Medieval Era? Give the date." Later on, students were expected to "Give the date of the Battle of Hastings, the names of the leaders on both sides, with leading incidents."

Third year tackled the rest of the English Middle Ages, the Renaissance, and Reformation. And in fourth year it appears that students reverted to purely literary studies, in classics and English.

Honours was different in at least one respect. It was more challenging, in terms of the level of detail expected to be mastered. Examinations focused on history and ethnology and omitted English. Like the pass sequence, honours students moved from ancient history in first year to the sixteenth or seventeenth centuries in their third; fourth year took them back to the ancient world, classical literature, and stray bits of knowledge such as the identity of "two early geographers who supply important information relative to ancient Britain," along with an opinion of "the value of their works."

Given the level of secondary education in the province, and the difficulties in securing adequate textbooks and ancillary reading matter, these humble questions may have seemed more challenging to contemporaries than they do today. Admission standards were considered low and, during the 1850s, university authorities tinkered with entrance requirements by extending the curriculum by a year, backwards, until they achieved a balance. Certainly judging by Wilson's first exams it is hard to imagine a student actually failing except through an effort of will: non-attendance at classes and a moderate knowledge of the textbook would suffice even for high honours.[22] At Cornell University, geographically and culturally not very far away from Toronto, fifty students were dismissed in 1868 when they incorrectly identified Portugal as the capital of Spain, Borneo as the capital of Prussia, and India as a part of Africa.[23] Taken together, the exams might suggest that Wilson at this stage knew little of his subject and probably little of his students. But, in the context of North America at mid-century, it is possible that Wilson and his students were well matched. In later years, he and they would improve, but some characteristics and some requirements were constant. In Daniel Wilson's world, facts stood high on the curriculum; presumably students learned them all the better because there were so few.

It is not easy to assess Wilson's qualities as a lecturer. One disgruntled student recorded sixty years later his belief that Wilson's lectures in the 1880s had been composed in the 1860s: "They were out of date, delivered in a boring manner and he as a student got nothing of value from them."[24] "Those who remember [Wilson's] lectures on history," sniffed another a few years after Wilson's death, "will have no difficulty in understanding how the Government expected to fill his position with a lecturer at $800 a year."[25]

As Wilson gained in experience, his exams at least became somewhat more demanding and extensive. European history surfaced in 1856, though in an ethnological context. Examinees in the late

1850s had to demonstrate rather more mental agility than their predecessors. In 1858 honours and scholarship students were asked, "In what essential respects does Modern differ from Medieval, and from Ancient history?" The eighteenth century (British, of course) took a bow, and Canada appeared for the first time. "What were the most striking events of the War in America, which terminated in the cession of Canada by the French?"

As Canada approached Confederation in the spring of 1867, students were invited to "contrast the position of Canada under English and French supremacy" and to outline the most important terms of the French capitulation in 1760. Nine years later, in 1876, Wilson (or his examiner, William Houston, MA) asked candidates to "describe the circumstances which led to the formation of the Dominion of Canada, [and] indicate, accurately, its present geographical extent, and explain, with as much detail as you can, the position of the Canadian Government."

Two years earlier the United States also appeared in examinations; and, as the 1870s drew on, there appeared the history of science and political theory, as well as Eastern Europe, Turkey, and Islam. Wilson's ethnological interests dictated the geographical spread of the curriculum and were much in evidence as long as he taught. Ethnology led history at the University of Toronto in diverse directions: farther, in fact, than it would travel again at the university until the 1960s.

Staff appointments also made a difference. History shared faculty with classics, which meant lectures from Henry Fairclough and William Dale, the professor of Latin. The arrival of William Ashley to be professor of political economy opened the possibility of teaching constitutional history; it also opened the possibility of conflict between political economy and histor for mastery of this important area.[26]

Wilson too travelled on paths more diverse than he would have wished. He was not granted his desire to return to Scotland, crowned with an Edinburgh professorship. He did not even retire there, becoming, instead, president of University College in 1880 and eventually president of the university in 1887. "So here I am," Wilson wrote, "President of University College, with a new lease of Canadian life; and the dream of ending my days in dear old Edinburgh ... all vanished into air."[27]

Though he continued his lectures, his attention was inevitably diverted to other causes: his unsuccessful fight against the admission of women students to the university and his opposition to university federation with the religious colleges. In between, he sought to instruct his political superiors in the provincial cabinet on the unwisdom of political jobbery in the university and the necessity of long summer vacations for professors.[28] By now seventy-one, Wilson found his extensive teaching a burden. While the government was willing in principle to relieve the burden by authorizing him to find a lecturer in history, in practice they were willing to offer a meagre $1200 for the replacement. The search therefore proceeded slowly.[29] Stubbornness and persistence advanced scholarship in other fields: constitutional law and political science found their way into the university with trained professors to teach them. Only history stood apart.

Wilson's final contribution to history at the university was an offshoot of the federation controversy. Dismayed at the failure of the 1853 act to bring in the sectarian colleges, the government decided to sweeten its offer. Against Wilson's advice it prepared new legislation that would make it possible for the religious colleges to carry on teaching in a number of subjects besides their own particular theology. These were classics, English, French, German, "oriental languages and literature," by which was in fact meant Near Eastern languages, and ethics. In 1887 the University of Toronto Federation Act passed the legislature.

The act divided Wilson's chair, history, a "university" subject, from English. He had to choose one, and he chose history. The curricular link with English was not entirely broken: it survived in the English and History honours course in which, true to its origins, English was the primary subject and history the appendage. The same was true of political science, or political economy, which surfaced as a university subject in 1885. Wilson worked to establish a new honours course in constitutional law and history. The best that can be said was that history was represented.

In Wilson's final years he achieved recognition, of a sort, from government: in 1888 Sir John A. Macdonald's government secured him a knighthood, for which Wilson was not grateful. As he told his diary, others of comparable merit were appointed to the various orders of chivalry while he himself was a mere "knight bachelor." Liking it or not, he took the honour and stored up a grievance against Macdonald. When Macdonald died in 1891 the university passed the expected resolutions of condolence and appreciation, while Wilson confined his personal opinion to his diary.[30] Macdonald, he wrote, was "a clever, most unprincipled party leader [who] had developed a system of political corruption that has demoralized the country. Its evil effects will long survive him."[31]

Wilson did not. Half blind, increasingly feeble, he had to bear the strain of a disastrous fire at University College in 1890 in which 33,000 books, not to mention the president's cherished lecture notes, perished. Wilson set about reconstructing the library (the government dropped the tariff on imported books for the occasion) and rewriting his notes, but the effort was too much. As he wrote, "the old spirit is wanting," and he did not have time, at seventy-five, to refine the product as he would have wished.[32]

One possible side-effect of the fire was to cause a major reorganization of course offerings, with the classicists William Dale and Fairclough taking a much more prominent role than before. The next year, 1891, witnessed the appearance of a course in both history and political science, with its accompanying "department" – the staff responsible for an honours course being held to constitute a department. Wilson died in harness, still professor and president, in August 1892.

It was Sir Daniel Wilson who established history, and much more besides, at the University of Toronto. He was the first to teach the subject, and the first, in 1887, to be formally appointed professor of history alone. He made history a college subject and then, in the peculiar University of Toronto meaning, a "university" subject. He bequeathed an entire system of education to his successors, a system in which history would be taught as part of a demanding honours curriculum in which the faculty were expected to exert themselves and, in fact, to make their principal effort. He was, in that sense, a true founder; having made a place for history, however, he had not as yet made a place for historians. It was Wilson's death, ironically, that did that.

CHAPTER TWO

Salad Days

S IR DANIEL WILSON'S DEATH on 6 August 1892 was not unexpected, least of all by himself. Wilson had been sick for some time and was trying, at the age of seventy-six, to resign when death overtook him. That summer it was obvious that whatever Wilson's immediate fate, he would not be able to continue his duties as professor of history.[1]

Wilson's decline, occurring during the academic dead season of the summer, when applicants were not easily reached and plans were already made for the next year, was inopportune. The government, through the minister of education, would have to make the appointment and, under the circumstances, the minister took a prudent course. He advertised for a successor to Sir Daniel, but only at the rank of lecturer. The salary would be $800, the customary amount for beginning appointments and not Sir Daniel's allotted $2800, itself a scandalously low sum and below the maximum salary for a full professor.

Wilson's likely successor was spending the summer in England, at Oxford. According to Edward Blake, who seems to have dreaded being asked to take on the job himself, "my son in law, Professor Wrong at Wycliffe College ... has made history [his] specialty." "[He] has informed me that he intends to apply for the chair, which should consequently be advertised,"[2] Blake wrote on 27 July 1892. When, shortly thereafter, word arrived in Oxford that the government was looking around for a candidate to replace Wilson, and in a hurry, George Wrong seems to have received a garbled version of events. He believed it was Wilson's professorship that was on offer.[3] Rumour, unprovable after Wilson's demise, asserted that he was Wilson's own choice of a replacement. Whatever the truth of that story, others besides Wilson were keen on Wrong: not merely Edward Blake, but Professor W.J. Alexander, the recently appointed professor of English, urged Wrong to apply.[4]

Yet Wrong was in a quandary. He had an established career at Toronto's Wycliffe College, where he was lecturer in church history and dean of the college, and a vocation as an Anglican clergyman. To give all that up and embark as a lecturer in history at the university was a sizeable order, and Wrong spent "some time on my knees asking God's guidance in the matter. I search my heart to ask why I shd prefer this sphere of work to my present one."[5] The answer, as Wrong wrote on another occasion, was plain: "No study ... can satisfy me or call forth the very best of what I am capable that is not the study of man ... I must study life, man, his cravings, his failures, his hopes. I am in short by temperament a student of history."[6] His doubts resolved, Wrong sent in his application – but for the wrong job.

Yet Wrong owed much to his "present" sphere of work. A poor country boy from southwestern Ontario, descended from decayed gentry, Wrong had passed from a career as a shop assistant in a Toronto bookstore, and hereditary Methodism, to being a student in Toronto's newly founded Wycliffe College, a bastion of low-church, evangelical Anglicanism. Simultaneously Wrong enrolled at the University of Toronto in an honours course in Mental and Moral Philosophy and Civil Polity, but it was at Wycliffe that he made the greatest impression. Graduating in 1883, at the age of twenty-three, he was immediately appointed lecturer and dean at the Anglican school, and it remained his base for the next nine years.[7]

Wrong became an active academic citizen. He took his teaching duties very seriously, and took lessons to improve his voice and delivery. He was concerned for his students, a trait he never lost. He discovered the pleasures of research and published his first book, The Crusade of 1383. He cultivated support for Wycliffe, and found it among the evangelically inclined business and political elite of the city as well as from Sir Daniel Wilson himself. The Blake family were especially forward in the cause and, before long, Wrong was a regular visitor at both their Toronto home and their summer estate at Murray Bay, Quebec; in 1886 Wrong married Edward Blake's daughter, Sophia.

The Blakes were one of Toronto's most prominent Liberal families. Edward Blake had been Canadian minister of justice in the 1870s and, in 1886, when George Wrong joined the family, Blake was leader of the national Liberal party in Ottawa. More to the immediate point, he was chancellor of the University of Toronto and, as such, an active force in reforming the university so as to make it a power in Canadian life.

Blake was a Canadian nationalist. In academic terms, that meant he and his vice-chancellor, William Mulock, another prominent Liberal, exerted themselves to make the University of Toronto Canada's "national" university and to give it a distinctly Canadian tone. Among other things, Blake and Mulock displayed a marked preference for Canadian-born appointments to the university faculty, and their views were sympathetically received in the Liberal provincial government.[8] It was they who defeated Wilson on the issue of admitting women students and reduced the character of his tenure as president to a rearguard action in defence of an increasingly obsolete past. At the same time, they extended political control into the heart of the university, establishing and largely justifying political interference in overturning mossbound second-raters. University appointments might have been ill-paid, but they were engrossing in a society that had few such positions in its gift and looked anxiously to see that professorships

were distributed according to the fashion or priority of the moment.
The system, given the size and relative simplicity of Ontario's
government and politics, meant that crucial matters of academic
policy, especially jobs, were openly debated and decided, and in a
political rather than an intellectual forum.[9]

There was a price to be paid, eventually. Opinion in Toronto, and
Ontario, was also affected by another current of reform that established
professional standards and condemned political interference and
political patronage. In the 1890s the reforming Liberal nationalists
of the Blake and Mulock stripe were evenly matched against the
"modern," reforming anti-politicians, but the balance was tipping.
Unluckily for George Wrong, who hoped to be a thoroughly modern
professional teacher and scholar, the circumstances of his selection
were tainted by the older politics. It is doubtful if Wrong appreciated
the irony.

Wrong benefited greatly from his family connection that allowed
him to move in the more privileged circles of Toronto society. His
social prominence and his political identification with the Liberals (his
parents had been Tories) did not work entirely to his advantage, as he
discovered when he applied to become professor of history in 1892.[10]
Complicated negotiations then ensued. The government was prepared
to improve the salary but not the title of the position. It seems Wrong
was told that if things worked out he could apply for the professorship
itself in two or three years, and on that basis he accepted. In the fall
of 1892 he officially joined the faculty of the University of Toronto
– in the Department of Political Economy because, as James Mavor
later pointed out, there was no department of history.[11]

The government must have breathed a sigh of relief. The university
calendar was rushed to the printer, noting the president's death but
maintaining Wilson's courses. Wrong found himself teaching everything from the fall of Rome to the confederation of Canada, and
including "ancient and modern ethnology," Wilson's fourth-year

honours course.[12] Some of his colleagues at the university looked askance at the appointment and easily attributed it to his influence with the provincial Liberals. The appearance of favouritism was confirmed when Wrong's salary became known: $1500, compared with the usual $800 for new lecturers.[13]

Appearances were deceiving. The salary took into account Wrong's nine years' experience at Wycliffe and his assumption of some of Wilson's administrative duties. It was in fact less than Wrong had made at Wycliffe. As for Edward Blake's influence, it must have been exercised at a considerable distance, for Blake had removed himself to Great Britain in 1890. Just as Wrong was being appointed a lecturer, Blake was being elected an Irish MP in the British general election.

The 1892 appointment to lecturer in history was apparently a success, especially for those who had endured Wilson's lectures; and all but a few of those who later criticized Wrong and alleged undue political interference admitted that Wrong was popular among the undergraduates.[14] Only Professor William Dale of classics put himself clearly on record to the contrary, arguing in a letter to *The Globe* that in two years of trial Wrong had not "inspired his students with a particularly high opinion of his qualifications."[15] Wrong was teaching in the shadow of Wilson, until Wilson's existing courses could be altered, and for several years he lectured on ethnology, just as Wilson would have liked, and adapted J.R. Green's *History of the English People* and Francis Parkman's *Wolfe and Montcalm* to the needs of his students.[16] Parkman's romantic and moralistic approach was in any case very much to Wrong's taste, even if he differed from the American historian on some details of his conclusions.

Perhaps Wrong's appointment would eventually have been accepted, but there were two other appointments in 1892. James Loudon became president of the university in succession to Sir Daniel Wilson, and James Mavor became professor of political economy.

Loudon was a graduate of the university, a medal winner, and professor of physics since 1873, the first Canadian to hold such an appointment. He was determined to reform the university by applying the model of German scholarship and by valuing research, an enterprise in which he enjoyed the confidence and co-operation of the chancellor, Blake, and, for a time, the vice-chancellor, Mulock. For obvious reasons Loudon, as a "national" himself, fitted well with their vision of a "national" university. But Blake's departure for the British parliament and Wrong's simultaneous arrival weakened Loudon's political position and stimulated Mulock's already pronounced talents for manipulative scheming, a talent that long after the event left a sour taste in Toronto's collective memory.[17]

At the same time, Loudon emphasized undergraduate education and the honours courses, which aimed to furnish "that intellectual birthright of independent thought" so crucial to an informed and democratic citizenry.[18] Loudon strongly believed that the best teachers were also the best researchers: according to Alan Bowker, "he favoured teachers who did research, as he believed that only such men could properly inspire their students with zeal for knowledge and intellectual exploration."[19]

Mavor was a Scot, imported from Glasgow at the insistence of the first, recently resigned, professor of political economy at Toronto, William Ashley, who had taken the road to Harvard. "Canada would be extremely fortunate to secure him," Ashley assured George Ross, the education minister. Mavor for his part was less convinced of his good fortune. "The manners of the Torontoese," he wrote, "are delightful, their customs are beastly."[20] Nor were Torontonians entirely captivated by the eccentric and autocratic Mavor, while Canadian nationalists were offended by the appointment of another immigrant to a post they considered rightly theirs. Mavor was a true Scot where education was concerned: a generalist, he preferred to deliver concepts as large as they were vague in lecture form.[21] That was unfortunate, since lectures were not his strong suit, in the opinion of many

students who considered Mavor a poor teacher and lecturer.[22] It did
not help Mavor's reputation inside the university, especially among the
students, that he intervened to prevent a debate between a Christian
socialist, Phillips Thompson, and an agnostic capitalist, Alfred Jury, late
in 1894. (It was evidently the agnosticism rather than the socialism
that displeased.) Free speech had its limits, especially on a campus
where Mavor represented the views of a number of influential faculty
and, possibly, the opinions of influential alumni.[23]

But it was Wrong rather than Mavor who inadvertently brought on
the crisis in the university. In 1894, at the age of thirty-four and after
just two years as a lecturer, Wrong was promoted to be professor of
history. Gossip spread: though the position had been advertised at the
insistence of the government, the president and his advisers had
already made up their minds that it must be Wrong and ignored the
better claims and seniority of the other applicants.[24] The choice, under
the circumstances, was not universally appreciated, especially by the
remaining eleven candidates, some of whom presumably considered
themselves better qualified for the position. And circumstances made
it all too easy to claim that Wrong had profited from not one but two
patronage jobs.

It was too much for some of his colleagues. Colleagues talk, and
academics can, on occasion, talk a great deal. With Queen's Park only
a block away, some colleagues talked to politicians and reported that
one of the ministers had confirmed that Wrong's choice was a put-
up job.[25] The *Varsity*, the student newspaper, was enjoying a burst of
reforming zeal and its editor, James Tucker, was anxious to test the
limits of free speech and unfettered speculation. Through the
grapevine he learned that Wrong's appointment was unpopular in
certain quarters. In the *Varsity* of 11 October 1894 he took up the
matter. "Certain unwise appointments have unquestionably been
made in the University," Tucker wrote, "and as long as the latter
remains to any degree under the control of the Government of the

Province we suppose political motives will, justly or unjustly, be attributed in such cases." And, justly or unjustly, Tucker proceeded.

Wrong was the least of his worries, an almost accidental example of the maladministration of the university. But if Wrong could be used as a stick with which to thump Loudon, then he must serve. On 17 October Tucker tackled the circumstances of Wrong's appointment, circumstances which, he alleged, cast a shadow on Wrong's very real qualities as a teacher and "a Christian gentleman." When the university council rebutted Tucker's attacks, he returned to the charge in a Hallowe'en editorial. One well-informed Toronto journalist, Hector Charlesworth, believed that this editorial was directly inspired and perhaps actually written by Professor William Dale, a classical historian and one of those beaten out by Wrong for the history chair.[26]

Dale would thereafter be at the centre of the storm, and his motives bear examination. Certainly his conduct was not always straightforward, but by the end of the affair he had demonstrated he had the courage of his convictions and, as a consequence, he would emerge as one of the two casualties of the affair. According to those who knew him best he acted not out of self-interest or disappointment but from a "strong inner conviction." There is no reason to question this assessment: Dale's behaviour over the months to come was fanatical to the point of obsession: he was better suited to be Savonarola than Machiavelli.[27]

The next week, on 7 November, the *Varsity* revisited the topic, this time in a heavy-handed satire entitled "A Fragment Found on the Lawn," which cast doubt on Wrong's testimonials. This stimulated further defence of Wrong's conduct, this time from his friends, who suggested that any criticism should be directed to its proper target, the university administration and the government, and not the blameless historian.[28]

There was a respite over Christmas, but it was merely a lull before a greater storm. Tucker was succeeded as editor of the *Varsity* by one

Joseph Montgomery, but Montgomery was soon embroiled in a controversy with the university authorities over Mavor's cancellation of the Jury-Thompson debate. So Montgomery resigned and Tucker was back, and with him the appointments controversy. The matter was evidently much discussed in Wrong's social circle. On 4 February Wrong's friend B.E. Walker, general manager of the Bank of Commerce, published a lengthy defence in The Globe based on information which only Wrong could have supplied, while Wrong himself, in an action he later admitted to have been unwise, took up the students' case in a letter of his own. Perhaps there were some staff unfit for their jobs: if so the remedy was structural, not personal. He advised the creation of a board of governors to stand between the government and the faculty in order to preserve the purity and reputation of the faculty. The students, he later wrote, had a real case to make even if their manner of putting it was self-defeating.[29] Wrong's attitude, judicious, fair, and understanding, would not prevail.

The following Saturday, 9 February, Dale responded on page one of The Globe with a statement for the prosecution, a statement that left nothing to the imagination and gave Loudon little choice but to discharge him, which he did on 14 February. He cited "conduct subversive of all discipline and in violation of the amenities that should prevail between members of the same faculty."[30] Loudon's judgement was, if anything, an understatement.

Dale's dismissal provoked a student meeting the very next day. William Lyon Mackenzie King, son of a law professor, who was also a student of Wrong's, moved a boycott of classes. Hamar Greenwood, later Irish secretary in Lloyd George's government, seconded, and with four dissenting votes Toronto's first student strike was on.[31]

The boycotters demanded that Loudon investigate their grievances and this, reluctantly, he agreed to do. The government did better: the whole affair was made the subject of a royal commission under no less a figure than the chief justice of the province. Meanwhile the students returned to classes, Dale sought employment elsewhere, and Tucker transferred his studies to Stanford, where he graduated a year later.

The royal commission served its purpose, channelling the passions of the moment into dry evidence and judicious conclusions. The conclusions, it is fair to say, were already obvious. Dale's charges in his letter to *The Globe*, the commission concluded, were mere assertions, not facts. Dale in his evidence stated he had the story of Blake's nepotism direct from the provincial treasurer. The latter worthy denied it, saying he was trying to reassure Dale there was no undue influence and he had heard Blake utter Wrong's name only once, and not in this connection. Dale had heard only what he wanted to hear.[32]

There were further lessons to be drawn, but they took time. The problem of university governance was not a priority for the Liberals at Queen's Park. Nor was finance, and as long as the Liberals ruled they turned a deaf ear to the university's importunities for more money. Any changes at the university would have to come cheap.

President Loudon's work was not done, and while the crisis of 1895 did not do much to enhance his position, it did remove a couple of the harshest critics of his administration. Mulock carried on as vice-chancellor, which may not have been an advantage as far as Loudon was concerned. With the victory of the Liberals in the federal election the next year, however, Mulock found a distraction, becoming federal postmaster general and minister of labour, in which capacity he soon found occasion to hire the young Mackenzie King. His war with Loudon was thereafter carried on at a distance until, in 1900, Mulock resigned as vice-chancellor.

In the meantime George Wrong carried on, professor of history at last, at the head of his own "course." Since every course had a department to teach it, he was also head of the Department of History.

The professor of history *was* the history department, but the history department was not yet a department in the twentieth-century sense.

Part of the problem was with definition, and definition was not helped by the fact that the term "department" was employed in two distinct meanings, "graduating department," the sense in which it appeared in the university calendar, and "teaching department," meaning a body of teachers in a given subject.[33]

The term expressed a phenomenon that may today be imperfectly grasped. A graduating department listed courses, had faculty, and met regularly to consider course offerings and student standing. Its key meeting was in the spring, when exam results were tallied and grades confirmed. Student rankings were then calculated, with keen attention given to the coveted "first-class" positions. To "stand" I.1 (one-one, or first in first-class honours) was a considerable distinction and one that was broadcast to the entire province, since the university's exam results were published in the newspapers. A graduating department thus had its own unity of purpose and function, even though for the purpose of salary or office its members resided elsewhere.

History became in 1895 a graduating department, not enough to clarify its identity or independence. The other part of history's problem was status. It was a part of political economy, falling under the jurisdiction of James Mavor. Wrong attended meetings of that department until 1905 and taught history to political economy students, among others, as part of their course.[34]

Recent events had removed William Dale from the History course and his successor was not immediately to hand. The government's niggardliness guaranteed that Wrong would not have much company for a few years at least. That was a trial, but it was also an opportunity, since it gave the new professor a uniquely free hand in shaping the teaching of history at the university, to become a second founder for the discipline. But what was history, and where did it fit?

The answer to that question was partly intellectual, but it was also partly territorial and, consequently, partly political, bound up in the toils of university politics. Though in 1895 Wrong's fiercest critics came from classics, his main rival thereafter was the professor of political economy, James Mavor. The battleground was constitutional history, British constitutional history to be sure, but it was also Canadian in an age when Canada, and therefore every Canadian, was British. The British constitution illustrated the advance of liberty in the world, and eventually democracy too. Its study was an essential component of the ideal of citizenship that Wrong hoped to inculcate in his students.[35]

The outcome of the struggle with Mavor would determine whether history or political science would shape Toronto's graduates, an issue at the heart of the university's *raison d'être*. The choice of weapons, however, was personal.

The two men were certainly a study in contrasts. Mavor was eccentric, even raffish, outspoken, and, on occasion, wildly controversial. His reputation as a teacher was at best mixed as he strove to inject his ideas into the political sphere. But while Mavor made less impact than he would have liked in the classroom, he was a major force outside, single-handedly securing the migration of thousands of oppressed Doukhobors from imperial Russia to Canada or, later, inspiring if not directing the opposition of private investors to the creation of Ontario Hydro. Tolstoy and Kropotkin were Mavor's allies and correspondents. His work with Russians stimulated his mind and his scholarship, and it is not surprising that he achieved a higher reputation outside Toronto than inside with his work on the economic history of Russia. In Mavor the university enjoyed a scholar of international stature.

Wrong, in contrast, was far better known inside the university than outside. He approached his scholarship, as he approached most things, very seriously. He exerted himself to research and publish in the history of Canada, and concentrated on the relations of English and French in the dominion. Serious as he was about his scholarly activity, it had to give way to his work as a teacher and public figure. While he was prolific, publishing seventeen volumes, it was not until 1928 that he completed his magnum opus, *The Rise and Fall of New France*, in two volumes. Unfortunately his work was dated before it appeared in print. "He let the best that was in him wait a little too long," Alan Bowker has concluded.[36] It is not as a research historian that Wrong deserves to be remembered.

Wrong also dedicated himself to advancing the cause of other scholars by founding and editing the *Review of Historical Publications Relating to Canada*, which turned into the *Canadian Historical Review* (1920). He created the Champlain Society to publish or republish forgotten literature dealing with Canada. In all these enterprises he advanced professional history in Canada. As in his own work, he helped keep it in touch with, if not abreast of, historical developments elsewhere.

Wrong believed he had a duty to convey historical insights to society. The best way to do this was to cultivate society, which he was, in fact, well equipped to do. Wrong could and did move with ease in Toronto society, with the Walkers, the Lashes, and the Masseys. Their world was his world, and to some extent their views were his. He lived among them and entertained them in his home in the Blake compound near Mulock's own house on fashionable Jarvis Street.[37]

Better still, Wrong had qualities that appealed and that sustained his position as a middleman between his elite friends and public opinion. As one Toronto businessman-imperialist, Arthur Glazebrook, put it in 1918, Wrong was "not a deep thinker, but a very effective speaker, and very well known all over the continent. His influence with the general public is really very considerable."[38] Wrong for his part was not wholly uncritical of his business friends. "Our businessmen are not as a rule familiar with other countries and do not study them with any measure of insight," he told his former student Mackenzie King in 1922. That, he implied, was the difference between himself and them.[39] There were a few exceptions, men such as B.E. (later Sir Edmund) Walker and Sir Joseph Flavelle, the meat-packing magnate:

they constituted the natural leadership of the community.[40] He could of course hope to influence and shape his friends' perspective on the world, and to some extent he did. He also communicated his, and their, shared values to the world outside. But he never became a political figure of the Mavor variety. That was not entirely his fault, and certainly not his desire.

As time passed Wrong did in fact meet a great many of the world's prominenti. An imperialist, with a strong Oxford affinity, he naturally consorted with both his Canadian and his British counterparts in the pro-imperial Round Table movement. Lionel Curtis, Philip Kerr (later Marquess of Lothian), and Lord Eustace Percy became family friends as well as political allies. Lord Bryce the historian came as Edward Blake's guest. At the Blake cottage at Murray Bay he met platoons of vacationing Americans: eminent Bostonians from the Lodge or Cabot families, and President William Howard Taft and his family. And there were, of course, the Canadians: Prime Minister Sir Wilfrid Laurier, his justice minister, Sir Charles Fitzpatrick, and his fisheries minister, Rodolphe Lemieux. With acquaintances such as these, Wrong could almost become an interpreter, a go-between for Toronto and its university in a wider world. It was an opportunity he would not have dreamed of refusing.

Cultivating business, political, and social ties was consistent with Wrong's pedagogical beliefs. He had a whig understanding of history and, to ensure that Canada continued unhindered on the path of progress, the nation required an educated leadership that would protect and advance capitalism and democracy, two yardsticks by which he gauged the maturity of a nation. The university was the training ground for Canada's future leaders. It was the responsibility of educators to instil discipline and appreciation of knowledge in their students, who would go on to affect the development of Canada. Similarly, if he could influence the views of his political and business acquaintances, he was defending the integrity of the nation, which he saw as "a monument to progress."[41]

Wrong did not seek to confront society. "I doubt whether the soul is after all much injured by the luxury of good pictures, carved furniture, comfortable easy chairs and beautiful rooms," he wrote to his student Frank Underhill in 1912.[42] Such furniture, such rooms were most easily found in England, or in the well-furnished mansions of Wrong's anglophile Toronto circle. Wrong's own homes, both on Jarvis Street and later at 73 Walmer Road, with their elaborate teas and uniformed servants, were an outward expression of this attitude.

Wrong expressed this in his personal deportment. He was always properly suited, immaculately groomed, pince-nez perched on the bridge of his nose. He resembled not at all the impoverished village lad he once had been. "His speech was for a Canadian a little pretentious," one of his undergraduates later remembered. "He feigned an English accent you know." That was not uncommon in his day as a sign of gentility – in the American eastern seaboard as well as in Canada. Yet he was "a fine man" and "a good lecturer."[43]

With the elegant and impeccably mannered Sir Wilfrid Laurier, Wrong could study the combination of character and progress at first hand. Most of the time the Liberal leader did not disappoint, at least because in Wrong he was speaking to the converted. Although Wrong shared his business friends' scepticism of politics and political leadership – shared, in fact, the "anti-political" tradition common among turn-of-the-century progressives – he nevertheless kept return- ing to the Liberal fold. His business friends never developed into political leaders and, after an excursion with Sir Robert Borden's Union Government in 1917, Wrong reverted to the Liberals in the 1920s, and to Mackenzie King.[44]

History, "the study of man," was the soul of Wrong's life and the centre of his system of values, the stimulus to his imagination and the spur to his work. History was professional, naturally: "the first axiom of sound historical study is that it involves some, if necessarily a very limited, dealing with original authorities." But history was inspira- tional too. The magic of history lay in its attraction to the uninitiated, as well as its ability to mould the young. But the present value of history, as far as Wrong was concerned, would be muted unless he could secure the key to the present, the capacity to demonstrate the link between the British past and the British and Canadian imperial present.[45]

Wrong's inaugural lecture in 1895 set out his view at some length. "English political institutions," he told his audience, "show the firm balance derived from a deep historical setting. We have taken them from their home, and placed them amid conditions entirely different. Our society has had little of the stern discipline in political thinking of the firmly knit English society, and our want of this training makes us prone to follow abstract theories." Fortunately, Wrong continued, "modern politics" demonstrated the futility of such an approach and so, of course, did history. As Paul Phillips has noted, "the indirect benefits of studying British constitutional history for a proper grasp of current Canadian developments were quite evident."[46]

Wrong coexisted uneasily with Mavor for an entire decade. Periodically the two scrapped over constitutional history, essential for the study of both political science and law as they were then construed. But they disagreed on other matters too, for example the hoary question of specialization versus general knowledge. Wrong championed the Oxford model of specialization, and with it tutorials, small discussion groups of students meeting with a professor, as the heart of undergraduate education; Mavor, by contrast, embraced general knowledge and concentrated on lecturing.

That did not prevent Wrong from establishing a distinctive History curriculum embodied in two honours courses: History proper, and History and English, the latter being a joint project with his friend W.J. Alexander.[47] The foundation of the history part of the curriculum remained a combination of classical, medieval, and modern histories, with Wrong listed in the calendar as the sole "officer of instruction." Change came slowly. Ethnology in fourth year lasted until 1901, and even afterwards the department continued to be listed as "history and ethnology."

The more Wrong had his way, the less Mavor liked it. History was a vital part of the education of undergraduate political economy, but history as Wrong conceived and defined it was far too specialized. The difference of opinion is reflected in a bifurcation of Wrong's offerings, between odd-numbered courses that progressed from medieval to modern (Histories 1, 3, and 5) and even numbered cognate courses (2, 4, and 6) that included, in third and fourth years, "special studies."

By 1904-5 the History course began with a general year, in which students were expected to sample English, languages ancient and modern, science, religion (offered in two forms, one for the religious colleges and one for secular University College), and Greek and Roman history. None of these subjects was taught by Wrong, who was reserved until second year.

Second year was the history of medieval Europe, "including the continuous history of the British Isles." Wrong felt it wise to inform students that "essays may be required during the year, and the merits of these essays will be taken into account in determining the standing in the class lists." Recommended books for the course included Lord Bryce on the Holy Roman Empire. There were two compulsory courses, History 1 and 2, the former being described as "chief movements" of medieval history, and the latter as "the history of Europe," but including anthropology and geography as they related to the subject.

Third year featured two history courses, History 3 and 4, dealing with European and American history from 1300 to 1763. Canadian history made its appearance under this heading. Parkman vanished from the reading list, but only temporarily, and was replaced by Bourinot's and Roberts's texts on Canadian history. Finally, in fourth year, students followed History 5 and 6, covering North America and Europe "from 1763 to the present time," plus the philosophy of history, for which Hegel was prescribed, though in dilute form. In History 6, "the continuous history of the British Empire and the United States" was treated; but a "special study" was added, either of the French Revolution or the history of Canada.

Besides history, honours history students were expected to take a heavy diet of languages, economics, psychology, ethics, and constitutional law and history. Honours students in English and history had by definition less choice, though they too were expected to master French and German and to continue their studies in Latin until the end of second year.[48]

Wrong was by then ready for the next step: the metamorphosis of history from "graduating" to full departmental status. In 1905 he got his wish, with the establishment of the Modern History course and the appointment of Edward Kylie as lecturer in history. Wrong no longer was a department, he had a department.

The Modern History course still displayed its origins in political economy. The first year it shared with political economy as "Modern History and Political Science." Then students enrolled, formally, in Modern History; over the next three years they followed the same basic chronological progression that Wilson had established, and Wrong had refined, under the old regime.[49]

If relations with political economy were close, they were not warm. Mavor recognized the appearance of history as a full department by excluding Wrong from departmental meetings. The new history department as Wrong conceived it was entirely unsound, he would write in 1910, because it "practically eliminated Political Economy from the course," which predictably meant that modern history would be "too highly specialized for an undergraduate course." That, Mavor wrote, "has turned out to be the case. Very few students have taken the course during the four years of its existence and the course has thus not been by any means a success."[50]

But that was not the only difficulty, according to Mavor. History insisted on teaching subjects such as economic history for which it was doubtfully qualified and in which political economy had a proven and successful record. History students were reduced to begging the time of faculty in political economy in order to cope with the demands of their own staff, and in any case Wrong's demands on students' time were so excessive that political science students taking a history course were overwhelmed. That was because Wrong's special subjects were handled in tutorials in which he and his staff emphasized essays. Mavor termed this "group instruction in subjects which do not form the principal subjects in the course which they are taking for a degree," a practice that might "result in wholly unnecessary expense to the University in furnishing instructors in response to an apparent but purely fictitious demand."[51]

With due allowance for bias and rhetorical extravagance, Mavor had grasped the essence of the changes that Wrong had made to his own preferred pattern of instruction. "It is generally recognised," one of Wrong's staff wrote in 1915, "that the introduction of tutorial work in any form is a challenge to the dominant position now held in the curriculum of the University by the lecture."[52] Tutorials did not, of course, exclude lectures. Under Wrong's system, tutorials were attached to lectures so as to allow students to explore the subject matter of a course. (In form, this meant replacing one hour of a three-hour lecture course with a tutorial.) Ideally, Edward Kylie wrote, "the tutorial system brings the student into contact with an instructor who has mastered the subject in hand and whose whole life is given to aiding and encouraging those who come under his charge."[53]

Mavor felt challenged both in his teaching practice and in his subject. He did not argue that Wrong might be choosing to emphasize an aspect of teaching where he felt more at ease than in lectures, though there is some evidence that Wrong's lectures were rambling, disorganized, and excessively factual.[54] Instead he directed his fire at a mirage. As it happened, Wrong had not much reduced the political economy component in historical studies. The real changes were in the regular course of study rather than in the less formal special subjects, and in the extracurricular structure that Wrong was building around his department. Supporters of the tutorial system argued that they were saving, not supplanting, the lecture: that small group instruction and large lectures went hand in hand. Continuing preparation and individual responsibility to prepare papers and lead discussions forced the student to concentrate on a course before the last, frantic cram for the spring examinations. But as Mavor suggested, the changes were demanding, time-consuming, and possibly expensive. They were, nevertheless, implemented. The Department of History thereby acquired a unique content as well as a clear form.

The entrenchment of tutorials produced a number of inevitable side-effects. Teaching loads increased. "If in a class of sixty students at present receiving two lectures a week it is decided to substitute one tutorial hour for one of the lectures, the two hours at once become eleven." Such a demand could be met by increasing, even doubling, the staff, though that was unlikely. In scheduling tutorials another principle applied. "It is a harder thing to give good tutorial classes to six students than good lectures to a hundred." That "is fit work [only] for the most experienced," not the most junior. And there was one final difficulty. There was neither money nor time to provide the same service to the general or pass course.[55]

It was as creator and defender of a system of teaching history that Wrong achieved his most notable success. He understood that the teaching of history in the university was part of a larger continuum. It was natural to try to connect the history taught in primary and secondary schools with the history studied in the university, and Wrong and his staff regularly appeared before the Ontario Education Association.[56] One of Wrong's future staff, W.S. Wallace, also wrote texts and histories for younger readers – a lucrative sideline for those professors who could bring themselves to the task.

Wrong's success and his system are best conveyed by those who experienced it – the students – in this case via a history student's diary. In the fall of 1903 James Kenney travelled up to Toronto from Belleville clutching an entrance scholarship to the provincial university. Though St Michael's College had federated with the university in 1890, the structure of courses obliged Kenney, a Catholic, to enrol in the English and History course at University College.[57] There he took the usual first-year mélange of classics and English, and returned home with first-class standing and a reading list to prepare for second year.

Kenney put the summer of 1904 to good use. As he proudly recorded in his diary, he consumed Bryce's *Holy Roman Empire*, Green's *Short History of England to the Death of Edward I*, McGee's *History of Ireland*, Pope's *Essay on Man*, Goldsmith's *Traveller*, *Deserted Village*, and *Vicar of Wakefield*, not to mention some Burns and Tennyson, using compendia of English prose and English poetry.

In those leisurely days classes started well into the fall. On 8 October Kenney inscribed the events of his first week back:

Tuesday I went over to Varsity and attended a couple of lectures. There is an immense swarm of Freshmen. I believe there must be something like twenty in Classics alone. I went up to Mr. Wrong's room [at University College] to see about taking history at St. Michael's, and found Mr. Kirby [Kylie], the Catholic student from Lindsay who won the Flavelle scholarship three years ago, there. He [Wrong] was very anxious that I should study under him. Wednesday he met a few of us in the historical seminary [sic] in the Library. We are to attend the pass lectures, one of which is to be given on Mondays by Professor Wrong on general medieval history, and one by Mr. Kirby on Fridays on English history. The honor work is to be done partly by weekly meetings of all the honor students in the seminary and partly by group work. We are to be divided into groups of four, and each group is to meet once a week in Professor

Wrong's room. Two of us each week will read short ten minute essays on topics set, while the other two will come prepared to criticise. The period to be thus taken up will be that from ad 919 to ad 1273. Mr. Kirby will deal with all the honor work.[58]

Kenney was sensitive to his position as a Catholic in a strongly Protestant atmosphere. Medieval history was not free of religious controversy, and the study of the Protestant Reformation in third year was fraught with doctrinal peril. In Sir Daniel Wilson's day the Catholic hierarchy objected to what they called his Protestant prejudices, and even twenty years later there were misgivings about subjecting Catholic students to the study of a majoritarian, Protestant version of history.

But Kenney's doubts were swept away in his admiration for Wrong and Wrong's system. The tutorial, Wrong explained, must be at the heart of university education from the first year forward. "He spoke of the approach towards a tutorial system in the fact that every member of the first year was assigned to some special professor who should be ready always to assist him in his difficulties."[59]

The system was not without its flaws. In 1904 Edward Kylie was assisting Wrong in establishing and teaching his tutorials. Kylie had been a prize student at Toronto who had gone on to Oxford, and, with Oxford in his background, Wrong judged him well qualified to join him back at Toronto. Initially Wrong wanted Kylie appointed associate professor, but, at twenty-three, Kylie was felt to be too young and inexperienced.[60]

And so Kylie, who had meanwhile turned twenty-four, arrived at the University of Toronto a mere lecturer, at $1300 a year. The initial impression was mixed. "Mr. Kylie has been talking all week about his system of historical study," Kenney wrote on 30 October, "but it has not materialized yet. Last week he was to announce the groups Tuesday. Tuesday it was to be Friday. On Friday he named the first group and promised to post the others on the bulletin board that afternoon or Saturday. It has not appeared yet."[61] At least one professor, Alfred de Lury of mathematics, remarked that Oxford's effect on Kylie had not been entirely beneficial, making him "over-refined and sterile."[62]

But Kylie, and Oxford, generally gave more satisfaction. Oxford was important, indeed crucial, to his work at the university, Wrong explained in 1906. He "thought that the spirit of criticism, so long as it was frank and well meaning, was a sign of health. He said that always prevailed at Oxford. The thick-and-thin loyalty of small institutions was a weakness rather than a strength in the ultimate analysis. He spoke of the great constituency Toronto had to draw from; the lack of this is the weakness of McGill."

Wrong proudly quoted the views of a visiting British academic. "Mr. Lord was a man of good observation and judgement. When Professor Wrong first met him he had shaken his head a little about the University of Toronto; he said, `You lack distinction,' a criticism which was very just. But two weeks later his opinion had changed. He then was disposed to rank Toronto second to Oxford in the British Empire in its potentialities, so to speak. He is a Cambridge man himself."[63] A word of caution is in order. Though Wrong deeply admired Oxford, he was never entirely uncritical of the place and was known on occasion to deplore some of its foibles: "its costliness, its snobbery, its class distinctions, its slowness, its complacency, its lack of contact with the real world, its over-indulgence in ritual and creature comforts."[64]

Over the next few years Wrong had the opportunity to give Toronto a distinct Oxford flavour. That was because the university had finally stabilized. In the first place its endless search for form was resolved, finally, by the election of a new Conservative government in 1905, bringing new attitudes and a refreshing lack of commitment to swinging economy. The change came none too soon. The university badly needed help. Its president was unpopular and weak. Its faculty appointments continued to be political baubles in the hands of Queen's Park. Worst of all, the university was broke.

The new premier, James P. Whitney, first sent money and then named a commission to investigate the situation and recommend changes.[65] The money was most welcome. Whitney attached university finance to provincial succession duties; as the revenue from death taxes increased, so did the income of the provincial university. The changes, when they came, were drastic, but also agreeable. The direct relationship between the university and the minister of education was severed. A board of governors was created to represent the province and manage the general affairs of the institution. A senate was established to represent the faculty. The president was handed additional powers, and his rival, the vice-chancellor, was swept away. The faculty would be given security of tenure and higher salaries, and there would be an annual provincial grant.[66] The federated colleges – by then consisting of Anglican Trinity, Catholic St Michael's, and Methodist Victoria – continued, and were matched by secular University College. The division between university subjects, including history and political economy, and college subjects, such as French and classics, also continued. All this was embodied in a new University of Toronto Act, passed by the legislature in 1906.

Whitney also promised that Loudon would be replaced; and he was, but not without difficulty. The new Board of Governors – prominent men like Flavelle, Walker, and the future Sir Thomas White, whose large houses virtually surrounded the university – struggled over the selection, fighting off the contending interests and prejudices that had clustered around the university. Finally, in April 1907, Dr Robert Falconer, principal of Pine Hill Presbyterian College in Halifax, accepted the post.

Wrong did not like the choice of Falconer, though the two were later reconciled. Falconer proved to be a mainstay both for the university and for history, but neither Falconer nor Wrong could have accomplished much without the newfound generosity of the provincial government, which was determined to make up for lost time. And if the government was prepared to be fruitful, Wrong was ready to multiply. If Wrong can be accounted the father of the Department of History, Whitney and Falconer were definitely its godparents.

The Oxford system of which Wrong so proudly spoke in 1906 was founded on extensive faculty-student contact. For such contact to occur, it went without saying that there had to be faculty to service the students. While history was still part of political economy, Mavor grudgingly doled out a fellowship for an assistant to Wrong, but it was clear that more faculty were required.

Oxford was happy to provide them, and Wrong to pay for them, though not very handsomely. (Toronto salaries were considered low by both British and American standards.)[67] There were Canadians — Kylie, A.G. Brown, Vincent Massey, W.S. Wallace (who held a regular professorship at adjacent McMaster University on Bloor Street), and G.M. Smith, all graduates of the University of Toronto and Wrong's special protégés. And there were Britons, products of a university generation that believed in imperial unity and the duty, indeed the necessity, of each individual to do his best in the cause. Wrong's British staff were selected and recommended by the master of Balliol College at Oxford: Keith Feiling, K.N. Bell, J.J. Bell, and Ralph Hodder Williams.[68] The British staff stayed for varying lengths of time, but all eventually left. (Hodder Williams, the longest serving, stayed from 1912 to 1923, when he returned to England to join his family's publishing firm, Hodder and Stoughton.) Wrong's department owed much to Oxford, but it was Oxford in a Canadian guise.

There was another aspect to the Oxford system. The mother university did not stress research or publication, and few of its graduates whom Wrong hired did much scholarly publishing. W.P.M. Kennedy, hired in 1916, possessed the only genuine research degree in the department; a Trinity College, Dublin, product, Kennedy sniffed at Oxford. Writing of Marjorie Reid, a female colleague, Kennedy observed that she demonstrated "a sound attitude towards research – sounder than one expects from Oxford."[69]

Wrong did not have an altogether free hand in the matter of appointments. The 1906 reforms removed the minister of education as the university's personnel officer, only to replace him by the president and the Board of Governors. Though Wrong usually got his way, there were exceptions. The president, Loudon or Falconer, laboured over the selection of staff, examined their qualifications, and, if possible, interviewed them himself. Fortunately Falconer shared Wrong's Oxford preference or prejudice: "We find," Falconer wrote in 1912, "that for History an Oxford training is most valuable. A strong Canadian or a strong Scotchman with Oxford training fills our position splendidly in such a subject as that."[70] Occasionally the board, or members of the board, also intervened.

The most famous incident of unwanted intervention occurred in 1911 when President Falconer was called on to decide between an appointment in history and one in political economy. History wanted a constitutional historian – part of Wrong's ongoing struggle with Mavor – and political economy wanted to establish a program in commerce and finance. Two individuals were discovered: Lewis Namier from Oxford, for history, and Gilbert Jackson from Cambridge, for political economy. Their curricula found their way to the president's desk, along with recommendations from each department. Falconer consulted Sir Joseph Flavelle, a board member and, as it happened, his next-door neighbour on Queen's Park Crescent. Flavelle was not so much in favour of Jackson, who had a mere second from Cambridge, as he was against Namier. Namier was found wanting, both because he was a Polish Jew (could a Jew teach British constitutional history?) and because he stuttered and was accounted unsociable.[71]

In one area Wrong was somewhat in advance of his time. From 1912 on there was usually a woman on staff, first Miss Winnifred Harvey in 1912-13, and then Helen McMurchie, who was "fellow" and then "instructor" (the lowest rank) from 1913-14 to 1917-18. ("Fellows" seem to have been the equivalent of today's research or teaching assistants.) McMurchie had been an outstanding undergraduate and prizewinner: she received the doubtful compliment of being called the "female Underhill" from an admiring teacher.[72] Wrong even championed a women's college (like Oxford's), on the ground that it would encourage the recruitment of female staff and might wean female students away from the study of modern languages to the study of other disciplines including, presumably, history.[73] The greatest champion of the idea of a women's college was Wrong's eldest daughter, Margaret (Marga), a 1914 graduate of Somerville College, Oxford, and an unpaid assistant in the department: the president had resisted an appointment, according to George Wrong, because of "the terrible effects of having a Professor and his daughter together in one department." Eventually Margaret Wrong's position was regularized and she was permitted to receive a salary.[74]

The other characteristics of the early department were plain. It was an entirely Anglo-Saxon institution, mainly Canadian-born, generally Oxford-trained, and mostly (but not entirely) Protestant. Kylie was the first Catholic in the department,[75] followed by Kenney and then Kennedy. Such appointments were unusual in a strongly Protestant culture, and especially in a city where it was proverbial that no mayor could be elected without the strong support of the Orange Order.

Between 1894 and 1927, Wrong was the only full professor of history on staff as well as head of the department. The headship gave him primacy among his colleagues, "my staff." They in turn called him "the Chief." But the staff were considered to be equals, Wrong's doors were opened to them, and matters affecting the department as a whole were thrashed out together in regular Sunday dinner meetings at

Wrong's home.[76] The staff, in the remembrance of one student from the 1920s, reflected the standards and behaviour of their chief: historians, unlike mathematicians, wore academic gowns to class, just as at Oxford.

The cost of history rose with the number of faculty. Wrong's style of life was affluent but he enjoyed unusual advantages, such as a fashionable house, courtesy of his wife's family. He presumably made some money from his publications, though it is impossible now to estimate how much. He employed servants, entertained frequently, and gave dinner parties. In fact his circumstances, if they are considered as a function of his salary, do not seem to have deteriorated over time. According to the Board of Governors, the cost of living in Toronto rose 50 per cent between 1891 and 1907. In the first year, Wrong was making about $1800 at Wycliffe; in the last his salary was $3360, up 53.5 per cent over 1891. Such a sum ignores any conception of career progress, as it would now be understood. Effectively Wrong at forty-seven was making, in real or constant dollars, roughly the same as he had made at thirty-one.

In 1904 Wrong, the sole historian, was paid $3200. The next year, with the addition of Kylie, the history "budget" increased to $4500 to accommodate Kylie's pittance of $1300. In 1906 Kylie, but not Wrong, got a raise, to $1400, and $300 was added for the occasional services of A.G. Brown. As the Board of Governors recognized when it took office, this was not enough. Faculty salaries were boosted on 1 January 1907, and raised again in 1907-8, in Wrong's case to $4000.[77] There Wrong stuck. He stayed at $4000 until 1919, all through the hyper-inflation that accompanied the First World War. It is small wonder that at the end of the war Wrong sold 467 Jarvis and moved to more modest quarters at 73 Walmer Road, a few blocks northwest of the university.

Coursework was expanding along with the staff. In 1913-14 history offered thirteen courses and what would now be called a reading course – the latter being an assignment to honours students each summer. There was heavy emphasis on British (or rather English) and Canadian history; but the United States formed part of a course in second year, France and Italy were studied in third year, and Germany was considered in fourth year – again as part of a broader course. The approach in British and Canadian history was oriented towards the original documents: several collections had recently been published by the Public Archives in Ottawa or by Wrong's own Champlain Society, and Wrong's students duly perused them. But they were still reading Parkman's works in their first year, just as they had been since Sir Daniel Wilson's day. Students in British history read the correspondence of Lord Chatham, George III, and Lord North, the Greville diaries, and Moneypenny's *Life of Disraeli*.[78]

Wrong was not shy in defining history to include the relatively recent past. Thus, second-year students in Canadian history read both Sir Joseph Pope's *Sir John A. Macdonald* and Sir John Willison's recent *Sir Wilfrid Laurier and the Liberal Party*. Sometimes old and new combined, with idiosyncratic results. In the spring of 1914 A.G. Brown's and Helen McMurchie's examinees in honours medieval history were asked to "Compare the life of a villein in medieval England with that of a 'hired man' in Canada to-day." Pass students in medieval history (examined by Wrong and McMurchie) were told that "the keynote of medieval life was co-operation," for which "the modern world has substituted competition."

The centrepiece of Wrong's historical academy was the Historical Club, which he founded in 1904. (There was an Oxford original, but Wrong's club was not quite the same.) The club consisted of twenty-five members, some chosen for two years (their third and fourth), but most for only one (fourth). It embodied virtually all the salient points of Wrong's ideas on education, and it was accordingly repugnant to James Mavor. The "so-called History Club," Mavor complained to the president, was taking up all the undergraduates' time. It was not dealing with history at all, but with topics in political economy – by which he presumably meant topics of contemporary politics or economics. He might have added that the club recruited its members from all comers, including students in political economy. And he might also have reflected on the interest and desire for participation among the students that his own department was ignoring. But introspection was not Mavor's strong suit.[79]

The breadth of the club's membership and the generality of its discussion fitted with Wrong's philosophy, in which history was a means to an end, the end being democratic citizenship. It was an enlarged tutorial, but, because of the audience and the special circumstances, it was a very superior tutorial.

The club's first meeting dealt with the very current issue of the European powers in North Africa, on which Kylie spoke. Subsequent topics included "Should the Railways be made National Property?" (1905), "Hudson's Bay and Labrador" (1906), "Senate Reform in Canada" (1909), and "Bilingualism" (1913), in which the discussants examined Switzerland, Belgium, and Austria-Hungary, presumably with an eye to bilingualism in Canada too.[80]

The club was theoretically democratic, in the sense that anyone – anyone male, that is – from any background could be admitted, as long as he had the requisite academic qualifications and met the approval of the membership. It met once a month at the homes of Wrong's friends, people like Sir Edmund Walker or Sir Joseph Flavelle. "It would have introduced me to an intellectual and social life of which I see too little," Kenney wrote, "and it would have given me an opportunity of showing what is in me before a larger and more select audience than I usually have."[81]

Kenney, with first-class honours in all four years, was eminently qualified for the club. When he was turned down in the spring of 1906, he was crushed; and when that decision was later reversed, he was exalted. His own paper, naturally, was superb, the best ever given at the Historical Club, according to a friend.[82] That may or may not have been true. One paper for the club, much admired at the time, was said to have been copied or at best paraphrased from a standard work on railways.[83]

The social side of the club is best captured in the papers of Frank Underhill, a member from 1909 to 1911 and afterwards a devoted supporter.[84] Underhill's calendar shows that the club in his day started off the year at Wrong's home, 467 Jarvis Street, on 14 October 1909. Its next venue was Craigleigh, the Rosedale home of E.B. Osler, MP, on Beaumont St, where Carlton McNaught, the son of the president of the Canadian Manufacturers' Association, spoke on the "Eastern Question" and Japanese ambitions. Z.A. Lash, W.E.W. Rundle, C.D. Massey, J.W. Flavelle, and B.E. Walker were hosts that year; Vincent Massey, a future governor general, was president of the club, and Norman McLarty, a future minister of labour (in Mackenzie King's government), was vice-president.[85]

No doubt the students felt privileged to be invited into the homes of Toronto's business tycoons. Once there, they did not find they were called to worship at the shrine of affluence. It was refreshing, one of them recalled, and extremely instructive to find his tutor, Kenneth Bell, "actually questioning the judgement of a leading business tycoon." That, Underhill remembered, "was another subversive experience in my young life."[86] Some of the hosts might have been miffed by such treatment, but the evidence suggests they too genuinely subscribed to the idea of free discussion and considered it appropriate in a university. Years later Underhill was to find that the connections and the practices the club enshrined were to serve him, and the university, well.

Wrong remained associated with "his" club, usually but not always as its first host every October, until ill health forced him to give it up in 1943. The club remained in existence until about 1974, and in its seventy years numbered among its membership a fair proportion of Canada's political, bureaucratic, intellectual, and economic elite. As noted, it may even have strengthened the elite by introducing "minority" students (Catholics and Jews in this case) as equals among their peers.[87]

Among politicians, members of the club included Dick Bell, minister of citizenship and immigration under Diefenbaker, E.B. Jolliffe (1930), leader of the CCF in Ontario, Marvin Gelber (1934), a future Liberal MP, and Vincent Massey, the future governor general who, with Norman McLarty, was a minister under Mackenzie King. Future professors were much more frequent: a partial list reveals W.S. Wallace (1906), J.F. Kenney (1907), G.M. Smith (1908), Walter Sage (1910), A.L. Burt (1910), Frank Underhill (1911), J.G. Althouse (1912), F.H. Soward (1920), Donald McDougall (1924), Lorie Tarshis (1930), Gordon Skilling (1934), David Spring (1939), J.E. Hodgetts (1939), J.M.S. Careless (1939), Gerald Craig (1939), Paul Cornell (1940), Harold Nelson (1941), Kenneth McNaught (1941), Paul Fox (1944), G.S. French (1944), A.E. Safarian (1945), Stefan Stykolt (1945), Harry Eastman (1946), John Meisel (1947), William Kilbourn (1948), James Eayrs (1948), Ronald Bryden (1950), Ezio Cappadocia (1950), Sidney Eisen (1950), R.L. Watts (1951), A.V. Tucker (1951), T.H.B. Symons (1951), C.M.T. Hanly (1953), J.F. Mustard (1953), David Gauthier (1954), Brian Heeney (1954), Richard Gregor (1955), J.W. Daly (1955), Laurier Lapierre (1955), Graeme Patterson (1957), R.A. Fenn (1957), Stephen Clarkson (1959), Richard Alway (1962), Robert Evans (1964), Richard Guisso (1966), John Stubbs (1966), Robert Bothwell (1966), and Douglas Hay (1967).

The diplomatic list is not as long, but still long enough. It contains, among others, Hume Wrong (1915), George Glazebrook (1921), Herbert Norman (1932), Leo Malania (1934), George Ignatieff (1936), Paul Bridle (1936), J.R. Maybee (1939), R.L Rogers (1942), Klaus Goldschlag (1944), Blair Seaborn (1947), Michael Shenstone (1948), Geoffrey Pearson (1950), and Vernon Turner (1952). There were, as well, assorted other public figures, such as Morley Callaghan,

J.J. Robinette, Sidney Hermant, Sam Hughes, R.M. Fowler, Frank Moritsugu, Alan Gill, and Julian Porter.

Hosts in the first generation of the club were Wrong's own friends: Osler, Walker, Flavelle, J.S. McLean, or Newton Rowell, the chief justice of the province. Later generations included Conservative MPs such J.M. Macdonnell or Roland Michener, another future governor general, Walter Gordon, a future federal minister of finance, Andrew Brewin, an NDP MP, W.L. Grant, the principal of Upper Canada College, J.S. Hermant, who was for many years the mainstay of the club, and other prominent lawyers, businessmen, members of the university Board of Governors, the president of the university, and some of the principals of the colleges.

The lists by themselves prove only that a fair proportion of Canada's future elite passed through the University of Toronto between 1904 and 1974. Once at the university, such people drew attention to themselves either through their academic performance or made their presence felt in other ways. Their mark was, in effect, made when they made it into the Historical Club, whether by selection by their peers among the membership or by recommendation of the faculty. The criterion seems to have been ability, for although the club was from time to time captured by cliques of one sort or another, it usually seems to have represented the abler students without regard (as far as a scan of names and careers will show) to their ethnic, religious, or geographic origin. Catholics like Kenney were readily admitted, and the first Jewish member shows up before 1914.

In Wrong's day it was a mark of distinction, and sometimes an advantage to one's career, to be noticed by "the professor." Edward Kylie, James Kenney, G.M. Smith, Frank Underhill, A.L. Burt, and Walter Sage all benefited from Wrong's patronage, either through scholarships or, eventually, through appointments. The Historical Club did little directly for its members except to bring them together and to encourage them to perform in a more challenging forum than they might otherwise have met at the university. It had few continuing links except its faculty sponsors and advisers. It was, nevertheless, a significant organization, integrating faculty with students, and, with the leaders of the larger community, creating and perpetuating an institutional bond between the university and the city. The university reflected the city, or at any rate the city's establishment, and the city's establishment in turn offered its support.

The students who were "noticed" participated eagerly. That fact should not surprise: most turn-of-the-century Canadian students (and American students, for that matter) regarded the university as an elite institution, as well as an avenue to the professions or to business. Thus a club that reinforced their connection to a larger elite seemed only natural and desirable.[88] The club was an alternative, though not exclusive path in undergraduate life, which at Toronto as elsewhere was dominated by social and athletic societies, against which even the efforts of Vincent Massey, the scholarly dean at Victoria College, could not prevail.[89] The club was not "professional" in the topics it discussed but, considering the small number of professorial jobs then available in Canada, a goodly number of its members did pass on to become professors even before 1914. For them the club may well have been a testing ground.[90]

The First World War was a testing ground of a different sort. Various members of the faculty joined the army and went to war, or at any rate to war service, during which they were paid half their university salaries. Hodder Williams, G.M. Smith, and W.S. Wallace enlisted (Wallace in 1916). Vincent Massey, now a lecturer in the department, became commander of the Victoria College unit of the University Officers Training Corps; Lester Pearson, a second-year honours history student, was his orderly.[91] Colonel Massey was secretary to Sir Robert Borden's war committee of the cabinet. Edward Kylie went overseas and was killed on 14 May 1916; he was appropriately commemorated by a scholarship that for many years sent Toronto students to Oxford.[92]

The undergraduate body was caught up in the early enthusiasm for the war. Drafts of students hurried overseas, hoping to get to the front before the war was over. That was not immediately exhibited in enrolments, which remained stable until the academic year 1915-16, and then fell precipitately from 212 to 126 honours students in 1916-17.[93] Wrong and his assistants struggled to carry on, with Helen McMurchie acting, by 1916, as his principal assistant, at $1100 per annum. Unfortunately from the point of view of the history department's interests, she decided to get married to a faculty member from another department, necessitating her departure in 1917. (She did serve out her term, several months, as Mrs Bott.)[94]

The Historical Club reflected the effects of the war when it took up, in successive meetings in 1915, "the Prussian System," "the propaganda of Pan-Germanism," and "Spiritual Germany." But in the same series the club also debated the topic, "Resolved that Russia is an untrustworthy ally for a free state," indicating that freedom of speculation was not quite dead at the university. Eventually the pressure of events, and the departure of male undergraduates, took their toll. The club suspended operations in 1916, and did not meet again until 1919-20.

The university endured the vicissitudes of wartime patriotism. There was a movement to close down the German department and dismiss its staff. In the history department, possibly as a consequence, the hours required to be spent by students on languages were reduced; French was reduced as well as German, and the requirement for first-year Latin was abolished. In some parts of the country even the study of Germany excited wrath. Wrong, however, maintained and even expanded his coverage of that country. Bismarck's life remained assigned reading for undergraduates, and a course on medieval Germany was added in 1916. (It was, however, cancelled in 1917.)

The great constitutional history battle finally came to a conclusion.

Wrong prevailed on the president to award the subject to history in 1906 and again in 1910, and then in 1916 hired W.P.M. Kennedy part-time at $750 to teach the subject. An Irishman, Kennedy broke the Oxford mould: his degree, a first, was from Trinity College, Dublin. (Kennedy was "prizeman" in English at TCD, and at Toronto taught English on the side, with a separate stipend from that department.) Eventually, in 1920, he moved above the salt at the faculty table, and became an assistant professor at $2750.[95]

Wrong believed he was well equipped to meet the war crisis. His broad reading in European history, his involvement in public affairs, and his wide circle of friends and activities all gave him a perspective on the conflict shared by few other Canadians. Nevertheless, he saw the war as an opportunity to bring Canadian citizenship to a higher plane through common struggle and sacrifice. "It is magnificent that humanity should learn to stand together on broad human interests," he proclaimed in October 1914. "The victory for justice will place our humanity on a higher level than it was before."[96] Nor was Wrong alone. As Ralph Hodder Williams observed in 1915, "I believe your staff in Toronto preached the true gospel of our part in this war, and preached it long before August 1914, as nobody else in Canada has done, and from what I can see, few in England."[97]

Wrong's prewar participation in the Round Table movement, a group of intellectual imperialists with, naturally, an Oxford nucleus, focused his interests and helped shape his attitudes as the war progressed. The Round Tablers hoped that the war would purge the British Empire of petty parochialism and move its political leaders to unity of action and, as important, unity of spirit. The Round Table promoted the rule of experts, the civil servants who were both above and beyond politics: servants of the state in a pure sense. The state they had in mind was the British Empire, given permanence, structure, and solidity by the war crisis, with Canada as a willing and prominent part.

This view was essentially the same as Sir Robert Borden's, and, as the war dragged on, Wrong discovered unexpected virtues in the government. Its dedication to victory and its commitment to sacrifice, expressed through the enactment of conscription in 1917 and the formation of a coalition "Union" government with conscriptionist Liberals, persuaded Wrong to abandon his habitual Liberalism and Laurier and to switch to support Borden in the general election that year. Wrong had already made the sacrifice: one of his sons was killed in the war, and another son, Hume, served successively in the British army and the Royal Flying Corps. Borden's retreat from partisanship was confirmed by his abandonment of patronage as a political weapon and the legislation of civil service reform, an achievement of considerable importance for university professors who hoped to train their students to a career of public service. Under the circumstances, Wrong's support of the government (in which Vincent Massey and Loring Christie, a relative by marriage, now served in Borden's office) was entirely appropriate. The conceptual link between the history department and a professional civil service was firmly established, though the actual connection remained to be fleshed out.

That said, the government did not reward Wrong directly. While the war was on, he worked to eliminate differences between Canadian and American academics, encouraging thoughts of a common background and culture – a useful but minor task, but a harbinger of the cultural diplomacy of a future generation. When the war ended, Toronto's professor of history hoped to join the Canadian delegation to the Paris Peace Conference, arguing that he had a special expertise on subjects like Alsace-Lorraine. Borden and Christie, who made the final recommendation, did not agree, preferring to rely on such expertise as the British Foreign Office could supply. Wrong did sign on in the Khaki University, which taught college courses to Canadian soldiers sitting in camps in Britain and Europe awaiting demobilization. While in Europe he met and befriended the commander of the Canadian Corps, Sir Arthur Currie (the future principal of McGill), using the opportunity to trudge around the battlefields, seeking his son's grave.

Wrong carefully studied the peace settlement that followed the war. The Historical Club immediately took up the subject and devoted five sessions to it in 1919-20. The next year Wrong offered a course on the peace treaties and asked his students to reflect on excerpts from the Treaty of Versailles, "noting carefully any large principles involved." Among other things, third-year students were asked to consider changes to Canada's international position as a result of the peace conference, the transfer of Alsace-Lorraine to France, and the problem of reparations.

Wrong got a raise to mark war's end – his first in eleven years: to $4400 in 1919, $5000 in 1920, and $6000 in 1921. Given the deflation that followed the collapse of the wartime boom, the raises probably restored his purchasing power to where it had been in 1913. His returning colleagues did better. Vincent Massey stepped off the payroll into an unsuccessful adventure at the head of his family business, but the rest, Hodder Williams, Smith, and W.S. Wallace, came back to promotion (Hodder Williams and Smith to associate professor) and higher salaries, $3100 being the sum for associate professors. Wallace moved off to become assistant university librarian, editor of the *Canadian Historical Review*, and eventually librarian of the university.

The postwar department continued on the same principles as before and, judging by enrolment, it continued to appeal to students. The combined pass-honours enrolment in history bounced back to 700, where it had been at the beginning of the war, and then up to 800. Some of the students in 1914 and 1919 were the same: the university granted them special consideration, and an academic year, for war service. "Intellectually," the biographer of one returned soldier wrote, "the University of Toronto and Victoria College asked little of Mike Pearson. Naturally, they gave him little as well."[98] Most of the soldiers returned to serve out their time and graduate, like Pearson, with minimal effort in 1919 or 1920. Because the government did not give generously to returned soldiers, there was no marked influx of veterans after the war; and soon the veterans passed and were forgotten. The real impact of the First World War on the University of Toronto would come in a different form and with a certain delay.

George Wrong was around to witness the phenomenon, of which he did not entirely approve. The postwar generation was fearfully frivolous, he found. Writing to Falconer in 1922, Wrong complained: "I have never known a year in which students have seemed worse equipped for their work or less industrious than during the past year. I am appalled at the disgraceful character of some of the papers which have been given us in the examinations."[99] But even in his own family there was a spirit of contradiction.

His son Hume and daughter Margaret joined the faculty after the war. Wrong exerted influence to secure the appointment for his son, although it must be admitted that Hume was qualified in any case. He taught the French Revolution as his special subject, and to an audience that applauded his vigorous style and acerbic wit. "I remember Hume used to have big classes," a student of the period recalled, "bigger than his father's." Father and son were sufficiently at ease with one another to allow for intellectual contradiction inside the confines of the Historical Club. They disagreed, among other things, about the spirit of the age – perhaps even including the problems of student life. "I remember Hume several times violently disagreeing with his father," Paul Martin recalled. "'Oh father, don't be ridiculous,' he would say."[100] Wrong's choices and preferences continued to shape the Department of History during the 1920s. He again sought out Oxford men, Canadians like his son Hume, Lester B. Pearson, appointed in 1924, and J.B. Brebner, son of the university registrar, as well as Ralph Flenley, an Englishman who had transmuted his Liverpool degree into Oxford gold. Flenley was admittedly at several removes from Oxford and already acclimatized to Canada; he was thirty-four years old when he came to Toronto in 1920, via the University of Manitoba and war service.[101]

Wrong remained a prominent figure in the university and in the city during the 1920s. He revived his interest in French Canada and, despite his support for conscription during the war, he veered back towards conciliation and rapprochement with Quebec. Henri Bourassa was so impressed with Wrong's views that he translated them into French for a generation that would, he hoped, avoid the divisions and antagonisms that had characterized the period of the Great War. And Wrong continued to publish, assisted by a leave of absence in 1926. Healthy and active, he seems to have considered running as a Liberal in the federal election of 1925. In the end he stayed on the sidelines, sympathetically observing his former colleague, Vincent Massey, who did run as a Liberal, go down to defeat and on to prominence as a Canadian diplomat in Washington and London. Massey at least could afford it. Wrong, who had some hankerings in that direction, probably could not.

In 1928 Wrong retired, but remained an active figure in the promotion of Canadian history and the various pursuits of a department that in many ways remained "his" department. Every year began with Wrong hosting the first meeting of the Historical Club. At functions and lunches the emeritus professor was much in evidence. Only in the 1940s did his infirmities finally catch up with him. Cataracts eventually deprived him of sight and mobility, but even then friends and colleagues, and some students, trooped up Walmer Road to see him. He remained a symbol of solidarity with the department's origins and its past, but also a symbol of its mission as he had defined it: a civic calling that had the promotion of Canada, Canadian nationalism, and Canadian liberalism at its core. Those objectives would survive Wrong's death in 1948.

Sir Daniel Wilson, president and
first professor of history

George Wrong, founder of the
Department of History, in clerical
guise, circa 1890

George Wrong, circa 1925

Edward Blake

The combative Professor Dale

James Tucker

University College in its original form, circa 1875

Sir William Mulock in old age

Sir Robert Falconer

Canon H.J. Cody

The youthful MacKenzie King

Baldwin House

Convocation, 1925, showing academic procession from University College to Convocation Hall

Edward Kylie

George M. Smith, chairman 1927-9

Vincent Massey

Stewart Wallace

Margaret Wrong

Freya Hahn and her sister
Sylvia Hahn

Marjorie Reid

Four Diplomats

Lester B. (Mike) Pearson

Hume Wrong

G.P. de T. Glazebrook

Gerry Riddell

Frank Underhill

Chester Martin

Donald Crieghton

Richard Saunders

Flavelle House

Sidney Smith Hall

The 1950s

Ralph Flenley

Donald McDougall

Bertie Wilkinson

J.M.S. Careless

Gerald Craig

J.B. Conacher

C.P. Stacey

The Historical Club
of the
University of Toronto

The annual dinner of the Club will be held on Thursday evening, March 17th, at 7.15 p.m., in the Faculty Union, Hart House.   The Right Honourable Mr. Justice Duff is to be the speaker of the evening.

All past members of the club, as well as members and members-elect, are urged to be present.   Please inform the secretary, Mr. G. A. McGillivray, 123 St. George St., if you propose to attend.

The subscription for the dinner is $2.00 for all but active members who have paid their fees.   It may be sent to the secretary with the reply or paid on the evening of the dinner.

Historical Club

kesterton ennis tarvainen dzeguze ignatieff gilday rae mccaffrey mickleburgh haiven

Varsity staff, circa 1966

CHAPTER THREE

A National Institution

THE UNIVERSITY OF TORONTO's Department of History had a particular and, many supposed, unchanging identity in the mid-1920s, as George Wrong's retirement approached. The founder was still present and his system in place. Tutorials flourished, the honour course and the Historical Club both commanded attention, and the faculty concentrated its efforts on undergraduate education.

A glance behind the scenes indicates that change was as evident as continuity. The older teaching staff departed in the course of the 1920s. The transformation that followed was not quite what George Wrong intended; it left behind a department that was different in emphasis, and perhaps even different in kind, from Wrong's intention.

Wrong knew this was so even before he departed. Many of the decisions that altered the department were his, though their effects lingered on. He might have reasoned he had no choice but to cope; but, in coping, he created a dilemma.

The circumstances, economic, academic, and political, were against the continuation of Wrong's prewar department, with its Oxford umbilical cord and its almost exclusive concentration on undergraduate education. There was, to begin, the matter of money. Wrong knew from personal experience the effect of wartime inflation on professorial standards of living. That was hard enough when taken merely against the background of Toronto, but the University of Toronto did not exist only inside the local economy. The history department demanded its connections abroad; as Wrong conceived the department it was difficult to imagine it existing outside the transatlantic framework he had so laboriously constructed before the war.

Still in England at the end of the war, Wrong tried to come to terms with the new situation. When Toronto's history professor attempted to estimate what it would take to feed the Oxford connection and keep it healthy in the postwar decade, he became anxious. The comparative cost of living between Britain and Canada had been inverted, and what was difficult enough for Canadians was very unappealing to young Englishmen of the type Wrong wished to attract. Writing to President Falconer in 1919, Wrong sketched out the prospects, and the requirements, for moving Oxford first-class students to Toronto. They amounted to $4000 a head, or more. But Falconer returned a dusty response.

Falconer had more problems than history to face. There were other departments with needs: science and medicine, for instance, and the cost of laboratories. There was a new government at Queen's Park, the United Farmers of Ontario. The UFO were not especially friendly to higher education or to the provincial university. Until they left, in an act of self-destruction in 1923, the university would do well to tread carefully.

So Wrong failed in his efforts to get the university to offer more than $4000 for first-rate Englishmen; gradually he resigned himself to canvassing Canadian graduates, frequently second-class, from Oxford. Writing to the president in June 1923, Wrong informed him that he had a candidate for a job in the department, Lester B. Pearson. Unfortunately Pearson would get only a second from Oxford when he graduated, but what choice did Wrong have, given Toronto salaries? "The conclusion forced upon me here is that we shall not in the future, draw very many men from England for our teaching staff."[1]

That conclusion also occurred to Falconer, but he drew a different inference from Wrong's. Why not look to the United States, where the president himself had once taught, and especially to the prestigious American schools on the east coast?

The question of the United States and American influence would recur in the history of the University of Toronto. To imperialists, Canada existed as a denial of the United States even if, under some circumstances, it might be conceded that Americans, especially the east-coast or New England variety, were not wholly bad. Such Americans, like Canadians, might hanker for Oxford and the tutorial system, or recast their colleges along the lines of Oxford models. (The donations of the Harkness Foundation to Harvard and the establishment of the Harvard houses are cases in point.) Such elitist practices were a comfort, but in the American university system they were nevertheless a minority taste.

More to the point were the great state schools in the United States, and the graduate schools that were growing or sprouting everywhere in the 1910s and 1920s – even at Harvard. Wrong took a dim view of the phenomenon. He disliked what he saw as the consequences of American graduate training – extreme specialization to the exclusion of the real meaning of history.

"The Americans pursue a very rigorous and, to me, very one-sided method," he wrote. "If you wish to see an illustration of it, look at the History of the CPR just issued by [Harold] Innis of our Dept. of Pol. Econ. It is a sound piece of research but it is almost formless in respect to literary quality and the text is overburdened by footnotes to an absurd extent. And this excess of method is what the American School of History glories in."[2] Wrong's example was well chosen: Innis's *History of the Canadian Pacific Railway* remains almost unreadable today. The Americans themselves had doubts on the subject of specialization, and the contrast between the University of Toronto and comparable schools in the United States may therefore be somewhat exaggerated. Taking Innis's work as typical was certainly an exaggeration, but it is important as a symbol of everything Wrong devoutly detested.[3]

Under the circumstances, Wrong was not enchanted either by the idea of hiring Americans or American-trained Canadians, or by the growing prestige of the PhD. He was sceptical that a mere PhD could actually prevail over the humanistic values so desirable in a university teacher. He was reminded of a dinner in New York in 1918 at which conversation had turned to the training of historians at Oxford:

A Princeton Professor, sitting opposite to me, said he found men from Oxford had to unlearn what they had been taught at Oxford before being of any use in an American university. Naturally I asked reasons for this remark and so did George Louis Beer, who was present. In the end what I saw was that the American training is directed towards producing a learned treatise, while the Oxford training aims at the understanding of a subject. While we are not copying Oxford here, our methods are similar and a man trained in the United States would not fit in very readily with our system. As you see the converse is true in respect to the United States. I do not think this closes the door, and, of course, we must take applications on their merits.[4]

As far as Wrong was concerned, an Oxford education, combined with an unearned Oxford MA, to be obtained after the lapse of a few years and the payment of a fee, was entirely sufficient.

Graduate work, however, presented a problem. It followed the prescriptions of the society it serviced, where an MA was a mark of distinction in the high school teaching profession and of learning and status in the community. So graduate work at Toronto had to feed a quite specific expectation, and, even under Wrong, it did. It was of a different kind from the Oxford model, though the end result, academically speaking, may not have been much different. Graduate work meant an MA achieved by thesis and course work, as in the United

States. Wrong had been supervising MA degrees himself ever since 1893. By 1929 there were eighty-two Toronto MAs, mostly working in fields other than history, extant. (An MA thesis could be, and was, as short as a dozen pages, and the quality, by later standards, was not high.)

A PhD was another matter. The fact that the PhD was not highly prized, or regarded as much of a qualification, in the University of Toronto Department of History may help explain why the department itself produced no PhDs, even though it was theoretically entitled to do so. As President Falconer wrote in 1924, "I do not understand how it has arisen that it has not been the custom of the Department of History in the University of Toronto to grant a degree of Doctor of Philosophy."[5]

The custom did not last much longer. In 1925 the department granted two PhDs, to W.B. Kerr and Walter Sage, the latter at least being a graduate of the university. Sage's thesis, on Sir James Douglas, an early governor of British Columbia, was later converted into a book co-authored with George Wrong and Chester Martin. Sage himself went to the University of British Columbia to teach, becoming head of the history department there in 1932. That same year the history department appointed its second PhD (after Kennedy), George Brown. Unlike Kennedy, Brown's was an American PhD, and postwar too.

All this meant that the spiritual landscape of the history department, its priorities and its composition, were changing. The University of Toronto was moving closer to the model and practice of its American cousins south of the lakes; and with the university moved the history department. The advent of the PhD on staff, and soon the hiring of the first American on faculty, in 1931, had an impact on the orientation of the department. Paradoxically, the department and the university were reinforcing their position inside Canada by such means. Few Canadian universities could afford a complete PhD program. That Toronto should have one, comparable to competing offerings in the

United States, gave Toronto and its history department prominence and perhaps pre-eminence in Canada. A provincial university was on its way to being a national institution, and the Department of History welcomed and encouraged the change. Canada in the 1920s was becoming a nation in its own right, while maintaining many (but not all) of its ties to the British Empire. Toronto was still an outpost of British culture in the new world, but it was no longer the outpost of empire it had been. And if its intellectual geography was not what it had been, its physical geography was changing as well.

Toronto was an expanding and prosperous town in the 1920s. Its inhabitants had to admit it was still only Canada's second city, but they would add that in most respects this was an irrelevance. According to the census of 1921, Toronto with 522,000 people lagged almost 100,000 behind Montreal; by 1931 the gap had widened to 180,000. ("Greater Toronto" also trailed its eastern rival, by 192,000.) Just over 62 per cent were Canadian-born, but of the 522,000 in the city the large majority were Anglo-Saxon – 85.3 per cent in 1921, and 80.9 per cent in 1931. It was a fact that impressed Torontonians.

They paid rather less attention to the fact that the next largest ethnic group was Jewish, at 7.2 per cent in 1931. That fact was reflected, in the 1920s and 1930s, by a change in the composition of the student body that confronted the history department. In the Historical Club, Jews found admission and prominence. The first to be admitted was in 1907, and others followed. Lionel Gelber, for example, was president in 1930-1, and his brother Marvin vice-president in 1934-5. That is not to say that the University of Toronto or the Department of History was free of anti-Semitism in this period, but it does indicate that overt discrimination was not practised, at any rate in the relations between faculty and students.

The composition of Toronto society, and the expansion and growth of the city all had a ring of boosterism between the wars. Montrealers,

English and French, sniffed when the subject arose: Toronto's social inferiority and fearful dullness were the inward reflection of its outward tedium. These were matters best discussed behind closed doors, if at all. At the same time, Toronto was the capital of Canada's most populous, and richest, province. Its businessmen were rich and determined to become richer – the natural leaders of a national economy. Toronto was an appropriate seat for such activities. It was Canada's largest English-speaking city and Canada's largest Protestant city, dedicated, many thought, to striving and success. Its university was Canada's largest, and its faculty the most numerous. They were also, at least in their own opinion, miles ahead of any competition. In the expanding world of the 1920s, the University of Toronto was set to make its mark.

A visitor to the university would have seen changes since Sir Daniel Wilson's day. The Conservative governments of Sir James Whitney and Sir William Hearst had been kind to the campus. Around its centre new buildings flourished: some denominational, such as Presbyterian Knox College, but some decidedly secular, in the bombastic classical style of the period: the vast Convocation Hall, the Faculty of Household Science, a gift of the Masseys, the engineering building, or the utilitarian but still grandiose mining building down on College Street.

Older houses still survived in pockets along St George Street, but that street and the Annex to the north were starting to lose their fashionable character. Sir Edmund Walker no longer gazed out over the campus from his home at number 99, though Sir Joseph Flavelle survived at the corner of Hoskin and Queen's Park Crescent until 1939. Their children lived in leafier surroundings, further out in Rosedale. As the old families moved out, the university moved in, tearing down or, occasionally, renovating. As the administration made new offices available to faculty it saved space in more central buildings, such as University College. And in 1924 it was the history department's turn to move on.

It travelled the best part of two blocks, down to the corner of College and St George. There, on the northeast corner, was a vestige of an earlier and more spacious era, a lot 390 feet by 198. In the middle, facing College, was what recent generations of Torontonians knew as the Beardmore house, a verandahed mansion built in 1860 by F.W. Cumberland, a prominent Toronto architect, engineer, and railway promoter. Cumberland had bought the property from the Baldwins, who in turn had got it from the Russells, another prominent and privileged family in the Upper Canadian elite. Cumberland called his creation Pendarves, but the name did not stick. The building survived, intact and gracious, into the twentieth century. When the province required a suitable residence for its lieutenant-governor, it leased Cumberland House from the Beardmores from 1912 to 1915.

The end of the war in 1919 also marked the end of the Beardmores. The house was converted to a vocational workshop retraining handicapped veterans, Vet-Craft Shoes. When that closed, in 1923, the university purchased the property from the Beardmore estate for the large sum, in those days, of $210,000.[6] On the outside the house had been stripped of its spacious verandahs and its conservatory, but inside it was more or less intact. Thither the history department migrated in the fall of 1924 under the anxious eye of George Wrong and the university's superintendent of physical plant, Colonel LePan. Because of its greater historical resonance the name Baldwin was chosen for the building, even though no Baldwin had built it or even owned it. Baldwin House it became.

Baldwin House boasted three floors, plus basement. Thanks to additions and alterations, it had upwards of thirty rooms, three of which, on the ground floor, were of splendid proportions. But in less splendid classroom terms, three rooms could seat between forty and sixty students, and perhaps more. In the centre was a spacious hallway running the length of the house. Off the centre hall there ran a carved wooden staircase ascending under a skylight. On the second floor were beautiful and spacious offices, one of which went to George Wrong.

The building was shared with political economy for a number of years, until political economy in turn moved to the old McMaster College buildings on Bloor Street when McMaster transferred itself to Hamilton. The intervening nine years were not pleasant. "The office accommodation is most inadequate," wrote J.E. Urwick, head of political economy, in 1929, "and the inadequacy is the cause of great confusion and waste of time."[7] Ten political economists and eight historians coexisted uneasily, with history gradually expanding its presence as the decade wore on. Because the building accommodated teaching as well as offices, the confusion was amplified as students milled around the corridors and lounged against the walls, sometimes, to LePan's indignation, smoking. He was less concerned about the effect on health than for the effect on the university's insurance rates. Wrong appealed for coatracks and benches, with but slight success.[8] The fact that lectures were held on the premises was socially important: most faculty activity was concentrated and, to some extent, shared. Since the professoriate often taught in one another's courses and were certainly not confined to any particular specialty, such an interchange became crucial and binding. It was a stable structure whose members had an assigned and definite place. "There wasn't any questioning of the system," Richard Saunders remembered. "You were part of it and that was it."[9]

The reader may be curious as to what an office consisted of in the mid-1920s. Standard equipment for all professors included bookshelves (up to 200 feet), a desk, a comfortable desk chair, and eight chairs, presumably less comfortable, for the students. On those chairs they would perch during tutorials, reading aloud their essays or listening to their colleagues, stimulated in equal parts by physical discomfort and mental activity. The total value, for insurance purposes, of the history department's furniture in 1929 was $950.

The change in geography was not the whole story. The history department in the 1920s embodied more than professors. There was a secretary to look after the head and type his letters. The easiest and cheapest way of hiring a secretary was to hire a female student (all secretaries were assumed to be female); this system, when implemented, proved to have mixed results. "I regret that we shall not be able to offer you the position of Secretary to the Department of History for next session," George Wrong wrote to a St Hilda's student in 1926. "We feel that you would be very useful as Secretary, but we also feel that we must have a trained and expert typist."[10]

The perfect secretary was eventually found in Miss Freya Hahn, who had arrived by the end of the 1920s and stayed until the early 1960s. Miss Hahn held a BA in languages, but her qualifications were as Wrong had stipulated: typing and office management. She was also the only woman in the pay of the department, which could have unusual results. Richard Saunders, who joined the department in 1931, remembered that in his first tutorial he called on a young woman to present her paper. She stood up, fumbled with her script, and fainted. "I picked her up," Saunders continued, "and proceeded with her up the stairs to Miss Hahn's office, and there deposited her."[11]

The department depended on Miss Hahn, and gradually its life came to encircle her desk. "Quite plainly the history department was a small operation," according to Saunders, "and that was a good thing." Miss Hahn could easily know everyone's idiosyncracies, and in a small group she became, especially with Wrong retired, its centre. She did all the typing for the whole department, but she did more besides. In John Cairns's view, "she was considerably more important than most members of the staff. In her heyday, she was just about perfect in her role, calm, collected, committed beyond duty or (almost certainly) salary, knowing where everything was and what should be done, indispensable, the model of a confidential secretary to the Head ... She had the secret of being at once direct, impersonally friendly, and immensely dignified."

Miss Hahn made tea for the members of the department, but she did more: she in fact dominated the tea ceremony. Teatime had its function as a time and place of meeting. Sometimes members of the department used it as an occasion to spray each other "with shot and shell," leaving Miss Hahn "just a shade reproachfully aloof." She, as much as they, helped keep the department, most of the time, a small closely knit group.[12]

Miss Hahn was the point of contact between the department and its students, both undergraduate and graduate. There were more of the latter in the later 1920s and 1930s, once Sage and Kerr had passed through. The next doctorate, Arthur Dorland's, came in 1927. It had as its subject the history of the Society of Friends (Quakers) in Canada and was supervised by George Wrong. Dorland was already a professor and head of department, at the University of Western Ontario. And it was from Western that the next Toronto doctoral student, J.J. Talman, came in 1927, at the age of twenty-three.

Talman in 1973 recorded his experiences at Toronto in answer to an inquiry from the university historian, Robin Harris. In doing so, he answered, at least in part, Falconer's question about the department's customs in dealing with PhDs. Talman had the impression that the department wanted little to do with him. MAS were all very well, but PhDs were a burden. Surely Talman would wish to go elsewhere? Only George Brown, one of the most recently appointed faculty members, seemed glad to see him; but of course Brown by then had the only PhD in the department − Kennedy had left − and understood how the American PhD system worked. Fortunately Stewart Wallace, who ran graduate history, was also in favour, and Talman was able to wave a copy of the calendar, which boasted that Toronto did indeed offer the degree of PhD.

As it had to. The university did not after all exist in a vacuum with only Oxford for company. It lived in North America, and in an age when professional qualification was becoming more important. The appearance of Talman, and people like him, signalled a departure from Oxford that would never entirely be recouped.[13]

Talman later reminisced that he had got into Toronto by promising he would go elsewhere – the United States – after a year. Talman's idea was to work on Upper Canada, in the broad context of the movement of population and institutions across North America. None of this, he remembered, appealed to Chester Martin, but Martin found it hard to resist. "Since there was an end of my presence in sight, Chester Martin [by then the department head] was reconciled."

The shape of the PhD has changed very little. As Wrong and Martin knew, it was constructed on lines familiar to, even identical with, the United States. First there was course work, divided into fields, which in the late 1920s meant a major, a minor, and an outside (extra-departmental) field. Following examination, the candidate proceeded to a thesis. Two languages were demanded, even for Canadian history.

Talman beavered along, passing French even if his knowledge was judged imperfect: "How was I to know that the little animals in the hedgerows were conies?" Then he passed the fields. Historiography was compulsory: under Ralph Flenley, Talman studied Guicciardini and Benedetto Croce, among others; under Brown, in a proper graduate seminar, American history; with Wallace, Ontario history; and in a fourth-year undergraduate seminar in political science he completed his preliminary requirements.

Research was, by the late 1920s, differently defined from how it had been twenty years before. Wrong thought archives were a good thing, but not absolutely crucial to a student's work. Chester Martin had firmer views. Students must go to the archives. They must use the splendid new archives building in Ottawa. Of course, they must not overdo it. As Martin informed one prospective student, "The theses prepared in [Canadian] History usually require a month's intensive work at the Public Archives in Ottawa or in Halifax or in Washington."[14] He even established "our little research fund" of $250 to assist student travel.[15]

When it came time to write the thesis, Talman had no particular trouble with the research. Writing was another matter. Wallace, who bore the brunt of the work, was more interested in the research than its expression. That was something Talman regretted. "I do know," he wrote, "that I spend much more time with my students than Wallace did with me. I do not recall that he read any draft chapters. Certainly he would have improved the English if he had." A first draft was given a preliminary run-through inside the department and turned back, much to Wallace's disgust. That spared Talman both embarrassment and an exam fee.

The final act was appropriately impressive. The candidate defended the thesis before the entire university – that is, if the entire university chose to attend. Sir Frederick Banting, Toronto's Nobel laureate in medicine, sent a note of regret. Wallace, the supervisor, also failed to show up, explaining he had already approved the thesis the first time and did not need to do so again.[16] Talman passed anyway, and went out into the world just as the Great Depression was setting in.

For a department engaged in the production of PhDs, Toronto had precious few on its own staff. Kennedy had been the first, but by 1927 he had passed over to political science. The department Wrong left behind him boasted only one PhD, George Brown, a Toronto graduate (1915) who, after serving in the First World War, had studied at Chicago, where he had taken his doctorate. Both before and after Wrong's retirement the department continued to procure in the traditional way – among its graduates who had gone on to England, and Oxford, for training and finishing. These appointments proved more fortunate than Wrong had initially feared. Hume Wrong proved an able lecturer and helped out with administration as departmental secretary. Wrong's lectures, one of his students wrote, "were elegant performances, meticulously staged." Heaven help those who inter-fered with the performance: "On one occasion an unfortunmate young woman wandered into one of his lectures very late. Wrong suspended his discourse and with an angry and dramatic gesture, his voice rising to something like a scream, he ordered her out; she fled, over-whelmed."[17]

Lester Pearson ("Mike") was entirely different: "he had a cheerful sort of adolescent charm" that attracted students even if, on closer acquaintance, they were unimpressed with his scholarship. "On one occasion," Charles Stacey wrote, "when he was supposed to be lecturing on the period of the English Civil War he arrived with no lecture notes, but a copy of John Drinkwater's then current play *Oliver Cromwell*. He read it to us, and we enjoyed it. It was not a scholarly performance; but over half a century later, this is one of the few of the hundreds of lectures I attended at the University of Toronto that I remember with any clarity."[18]

The best of the professors, in Stacey's view, was G.M. Smith, who lectured with a twinkle interspersed with the odd apology for being "a plain, blunt soldier" (he was a veteran) and for using old notes for his carefully prepared performances. Ralph Flenley, the only English recruit who stayed, was no star: "of his lectures the less said the better." Ken McNaught, who studied under Flenley in the 1930s, took a broader view. Flenley was "a dear old duffer. Very gentle, very British, Anglo-Canadian, he was a terrible lecturer ... It put us to sleep in Room 8 [in University College] in the first lecture after lunch." Nevertheless, Flenley was "the heart and soul of kindness and *fairness*."

J.B. (Bartlet) Brebner, son of the university registrar, was attractive and capable in tutorials, but, according to Stacey, "the department was indisposed to encourage him." He left to do graduate work at Columbia and, when he was asked back, in 1929, he was unwilling to come. In a letter to Falconer he explained that as a teacher at Columbia he worked shorter hours, got more pay, and was able to specialize in terms of his courses, actually managing to teach in his research area.[19]

It was true that conditions at Toronto were less attractive than they might have been. Until George Wrong retired, his associate professors, Smith and Flenley, never surged above $4000 a year. Wrong, as we have seen, protested, but to no avail. But there were other problems as well. Wallace was sensitive to slights and in 1926 found an occasion to resign from the department so as to devote himself to his duties as librarian and author, for he was a formidable producer of books.[20] The year 1926 saw the appearance of his *Dictionary of Canadian Biography*, which for many years was the standard work on the subect; and in 1927 he produced a centennial history of the university. Under the best of circumstances, Wallace's work for the department could only help a little bit. There were not enough full-time staffers to go around.

That was the second effect of the 1920s. Inflation ate away at the faculty's standard of living, but a growing student population nibbled at their conditions of work. There was naturally a bulge at the end of the war as the veterans returned, but the university processed them as quickly as possible by counting time spent in the trenches for some of their credit. The total, pass and honours combined, reached 800 for the first time in 1927; after 1928 it grew again, despite the Depression, and never dipped below that figure until 1942.[21]

Smith explained to Falconer in March 1927 that it was too 'much to expect an eight-man staff to handle 800 students and thirty courses, including the "Teachers' Courses" (TCS) that were taught late in the afternoon for no extra pay or in the evening and in Hamilton for $300 a session. These were a heavy burden, and the results, in the department's opinion, were peculiar. Those taking TCS got far less in the way of classroom contact than other students, and as a result the standard of work "is necessarily much lower and less exacting." History was a compulsory subject in the TCS, the only one, according to the department, and attending to its needs tied down between two and four department members, winter and summer.[22] There were not enough historians to go round, given that burden, and there were other responsibilities too.

History was a department with its own "course." But not many students took that course compared with those who enrolled in English and History, or Political Science, or, especially, the pass course. History was therefore in some senses a service department, with an obligation to meet the curricular needs of others, most notably English. When English students were studying Shakespeare, in second year, it was natural that history supplement it with a course in sixteenth-century England.

There was also the tutorial system to be served. "Since the war," Smith explained in 1927, "all the Honours students in all our allied courses (except students of Political Science since 1924) and all Pass students have been seen for at least one hour a week in small tutorial classes ... My own belief is that it has been carried too far for our present staff of tutors and, for next year, we propose that Pass students be handled rather differently without less attention to the good men among them."[23] How that could be provided was a matter not only for the department, but for the president.

There was not enough new blood to replace those who had departed and it had become urgent to make a senior appointment immediately. Smith suggested W.L. Grant, the principal of Upper Canada College; W.S. Wallace, the university librarian; Frank Underhill from the University of Saskatchewan; Duncan McArthur from Queen's; Chester Martin of the University of Manitoba; Reginald Trotter; and George Wilson of Dalhousie (and a Harvard PhD).

As important, Smith urged that the recently married Lester Pearson and George Brown get an immediate raise to $3000 a year – "the minimum living wage for married men."[24] (While a bachelor, Pearson had supplemented his salary with a "free and comfortable apartment" in the Victoria men's residence, Burwash Hall. Married, he had problems affording a place to live.)[25]

Falconer took such advice to heart. He had changes in mind, even if not the budget to accomplish some of them. The first item was, happily, cheap: the very name of the department, which led to confusion (and possibly rivalry) with classics. So the department became Modern History, with its own course to match.[26] Greek and Roman history remained outside, in the clutch of classics, a necessary but detached part of a history student's first-year prescription.

Next Falconer promoted Smith and Ralph Flenley to be full professors, at $4500 a year,[27] along with W.S. Wallace; and he brought in Underhill, despite doubts about the latter's likely scholarly production, also as a full professor. As Smith explained to Falconer, "I was not confident that he would give us much prestige in the field of research in Canadian History but if this gap can be filled by Stewart Wallace, the prospect for a strong department will be much brighter."[28] All were in their late thirties or early forties, which gave the department a younger cast while simultaneously fixing its character at the senior level for some time to come. That was important; equally important, none of the four was clearly predominant over the others, though Wallace had an independent base as the university librarian.

The most immediate question was the succession to Wrong. Smith was in many ways the obvious choice from the point of view of seniority; he was well known around the university and Falconer liked him.[29] But Smith had his doubts. He had not published much, and he was still in his late thirties. W.L. Grant and Frank Underhill would make better chairmen or heads.[30] And if Smith had doubts, so, evidently, did the president.

When he came to dispose of the history department, he did it conditionally and half-heartedly. Rather than a "head," he asked, why not a "chairman"? And to guard against mistakes, why not an acting chairman? He put this ambivalent offer to Smith, who as dubiously accepted it.[31] The new chairman was told he was to consult his colleagues, the other full professors, in all important matters.

Smith naturally worried about his standing and his authority. He begged Falconer to make him acting head, in the usual way, so that his actual status would be recognized outside as well as inside the department. Failing that, he wanted an increase in salary.[32] But with or without the increase, he took the job, and with it a heap of trouble.

The first trouble was that there were more departures than appointments. Even before formally agreeing to become chairman, Smith was confronted with a direct consequence of Canada's acquisition of national sovereignty. This was a process that was generally approved by the Department of History, but its members had not counted on its side-effects. No self-respecting country could do without a foreign policy or a foreign service, and the simplest way to create one was simultaneously to appoint a number of rich men who could supplement their salaries with private wealth and, beneath them, a number of well-trained and well-travelled individuals who could manage the work. Prime Minister Mackenzie King paid off a political debt by making Vincent Massey, a former Toronto faculty member, minister to Washington. Massey, of course, had millions, and he also had connections, including a link to the Wrong family. Hume Wrong, who in 1927 was history's departmental secretary, was well known and obviously highly talented; and Massey appointed him, temporarily, to his legation.

Hume Wrong had no hesitation about leaving. He nearly doubled his salary, to $5000 per annum – more than any of the full professors at Toronto. Putting up with Vincent Massey, for whom his feelings were decidedly mixed, was a small consideration against such a benefit. He did not resign, however; the appointment was conditional and temporary. Massey would have to pressure King to make it official and permanent. The university itself had no choice, in view of Canada's need and Massey's demand, and it gave Wrong leave.

Wrong was on leave for quite a while. To replace him, Smith turned to the old stand-by of a Canadian at Oxford, in this case Donald Creighton, a graduate of the department in 1925. Creighton had gone to Oxford to study the history of France. Which kind of history he took in fact hardly mattered, since the Oxford experience, and the Toronto provenance, were what really counted. Reports from Oxford were favourable. Creighton was in any case in dire straits financially, and as soon as his appointment came through he wrote to Smith apparently to implore an advance on salary. In response, Smith gave him no joy. Interest rates were low, and a bank loan countersigned by Creighton's father would doubtless tide him over his last months at Oxford. "I am reluctant, at the moment, to appeal to the magnates," Smith concluded.[33] Creighton therefore began his university service in debt and quite possibly disgruntled.

His security of appointment depended on Wrong staying away. It was not an entirely comforting consideration, but it was at least better than the anguish felt by those still outside the charmed circle of employment.

Donald McDougall was such a one. McDougall was a veteran who took his degree from the University of Toronto in 1925, at the age of thirty-two. He wanted to pursue an academic career and took the boat for Oxford. This was unusual, though not unique. Wrong's children, Pearson, Smith, and Underhill, before the war, had done the same. But McDougall, as a result of war injuries, was blind. His perseverance in an age when the handicapped were expected to accept their lot and weave baskets in sheltered workshops was outstanding and, by the mid-1920s, well known. McDougall was being trained as a masseur, an occupation deemed suitable for the blind, when he met George Smith on the street. One thing led to another, and to Smith urging McDougall to apply his disability pension to a univesity education. This he did, subsequently winning a Rhodes Scholarship and taking a first at Oxford. All this was considered remarkable, but contemporaries considered another trait equally remarkable: he was a Catholic.

Toronto was not merely a Protestant city, it was inclined to actively dislike Roman Catholics. The history department had in fact appointed well-known Catholics in the past – Kylie being the most notable example – but in the late 1920s there were none in the department. McDougall let it be known that he wanted an appointment and was disappointed at the failure of the University of Toronto to offer him one. He mobilized his archbishop, Neil McNeill, and began a plan of campaign to get the post. Falconer was annoyed, naturally enough,[34] but McDougall's credentials were also appealing. In the meantime, more time and a fellowship at Oxford were indicated. So McDougall watched anxiously from afar. If Creighton did well, would that mean his own chances would be blighted?[35]

Another change was in the offing. Mike Pearson was scenting which way the wind blew. He was popular and easy-going, but he was not a scholar. He listened attentively to the advice of his colleagues, and George Wrong, that he should do something of a scholarly nature, and in the summer of 1926 he dutifully set off for the Public Archives in Ottawa. But he got there amid a political crisis and an old family friend, J.S. Woodsworth, the socialist MP, entertained him with tales of Mackenzie King. The research never quite got off the ground. Before he left Ottawa he attended a banquet at the Country Club, where he sat beside the undersecretary for external affairs, O.D. Skelton. It took some time for this slight connection to bear fruit, but, eventually, in the winter of 1927-8, it did.

When he got back to Toronto, Pearson gave vent to his feelings by writing a satirical essay, "The New History," for a student magazine. He mocked the "revisionism" of historians in the 1920s, and, in a sample essay introduction, urged the case of "Nero, a Hero."[36]

The catalyst to Pearson's departure was W.P.M. Kennedy, the constitutional historian, who had moved to political science but maintained a close interest in his old department. He wrote to Skelton on Pearson's behalf, and seems to have urged his younger colleague to be realistic. Mike was no scholar and he was surrounded by others who were, including the most recently arrived, Creighton. In May

Pearson applied to write the entrance exams for the Department of External Affairs, using Falconer, Kennedy, and Newton Rowell, the province's chief justice, as his references. He placed first, and in August a job offer followed.[37] G.M. Smith, who was on vacation, later told Falconer what happened: "On Friday last, I had a wire from Hume Wrong stating that he had resigned; on Sunday, I learned from Lester Pearson that the Civil Service Commision had placed him first in big field in the examination for a first secretaryship."[38] Pearson would be missed; with him went the faculty's closest link with the undergraduates and their youthful social world. Pearson had already married a student, Maryon Moody of Winnipeg, like himself a graduate of Victoria College.

As Hume Wrong's departure was Creighton's opportunity, so Pearson's farewell the next year was the salvation of Edgar McInnis. McInnis was another Toronto BA, a Rhodes Scholar (1923) who, after his time at Oxford, took a post at Oberlin College in Ohio, Toronto not then having anything to offer.[39] McDougall not being available (he had a fellowship and was settled for the year at Oxford), Smith turned to McInnis, who accepted, at $1800 a year, far less than Pearson had been making. The low salary is striking enough, but another point should be made: the recommendation of McInnis, Falconer was told, was the unanimous desire of the members of the department then present in Toronto. Falconer did not demur. Subject to budget, it would appear, the department had achieved a considerably greater degree of autonomy than it had once enjoyed; and, given the time constraints, it proved able to act efficiently on its own behalf.[40]

McDougall came the next year, 1929, at $2000. Tradition later held that he was the first and only Catholic the department hired for many years. That was not true, though it did speak to the department's reputation and, as the legend persisted and grew, to its own opinion of itself. In 1929 McDougall was not the only appointment, or the most notable. On 12 April President Falconer wrote to Professor

Chester Martin of the University of Manitoba, offering to make him full professor and head of the department, at a salary of $5500. A few days earlier, Falconer had formalized the resignation of G.M. Smith, as professor and chairman.

Very little is known about Smith's departure. In his letter of resignation, he referred to "the difficult period preceding my decision to resign" and thanked Falconer for his understanding and tolerance. He stayed in Toronto for a few years, "in business," attended an international relations conference in China in 1931, and then resumed his academic career as professor and head of history at the University of Alberta in Edmonton. He died in 1947, at the age of fifty-nine.

The succession was Chester Martin's. Martin would be head of the department for twenty-four years, the longest tenure after Wrong's; and apart from Wrong he was its only "head." His reputation had been made far away from Toronto, in the Maritimes, from which he hailed, and at Oxford, where he was the first Rhodes Scholar, in 1904. He then founded the University of Manitoba's history department in 1909, and taught there for twenty years before moving to Toronto.

His view of history was, as Carl Berger has indicated, complex. Canada was far from being a historically self-sufficient entity but was part of a larger transatlantic whole that included Great Britain and France as well as the United States. There were no inevitabilities, no large structures, in Martin's view of the world; "wiser counsels and better men" made the difference in history, and not impersonal fate. At the centre of his interests was Canada's constitutional evolution.[41]

"Seemly reticence" governed Martin's approach to some aspects of his subject, and "seemly reticence" would have governed the life of the history department if its head had been able entirely to have his way. As Donald Creighton later remarked, "Chester Martin was notoriously very secretive about departmental politics." That was different from Wrong's time, when problems were anticipated and shared among the professor and his junior colleagues. Yet Martin was kindly and he had a presence of his own – "Nova Scotian dignity," according to one colleague.[42]

The emphasis on propriety was not new and was reinforced by changes at the top of the university, where Sir Robert Falconer, after twenty-five years, retired in 1932, at the age of sixty-five. His successor, Canon Henry John Cody, was an Anglican clergyman, a sometime Conservative politician and minister of education in 1918-19, longtime member of the Board of Governors, and, finally, its chairman from 1923 to 1932. Cody was just a year younger than Falconer, but time had not dimmed his ambitions and experience had not much altered his outlook.[43] His connections with Toronto's business elite and with the Conservative party were close. In Cody's world, the university was not only a part of a larger society but one of its bulwarks.

That might have been seen as a continuation of the era of George Wrong, in which the history department was a part, and a respectable part, of the life of Toronto society, a time in which financial problems were solved, if possible, by an appeal to the money of the city's "magnates." But under Wrong there was a difference: the old professor put a premium on freedom of speech and the exchange of ideas, and his Historical Club had brought university life into reciprocal contact with the city and the society it served. The reciprocal character of the club, its relationship with its respectable hosts and the vigour of its discussions, should be underlined. That continued to be true in the 1930s, when such topics as "This Club would welcome the accession of the CCF to power," or "In the opinion of the Club the class struggle has been the most decisive factor in the growth of western civilization" were aired. These were topics not frequently heard in Toronto salons, but they were typical of the intellectual climate of the university, where the failures of the existing economic and political order were frequently voiced – in private.

The club continued to be for males only, a very odd development in a period when more than half the students in the three honour courses of English and History, Modern History, and Philosophy (English or History) were women. (It was also a period in which women did not fail to win "firsts" in their courses.)[44] Attending the club and its discussions were members of the department, including Frank Underhill, an old member but in the 1930s a leading light in the new socialist CFF party. Unfortunately for its sedate figurehead, the history department was headed into stormy waters.

The 1930s were not placid. The Great Depression hit Canada and Ontario hard. Provincial revenues plummetted, and with them the province's ability to finance its several burdens, including its university system. The nadir was reached at the end of 1932 or the beginning of 1933, but not all industries or regions were affected consistently or equally. The economy expanded after 1933, with a consequent easing of fiscal burdens for the provincial government. Economy was called for, nevertheless, both under the Conservatives, in power until 1934, and the Liberals thereafter. Indeed, the Liberal premier Mitchell Hepburn (1934-42) made something of a fetish of budget cuts and ostentatious economies; fortunately for the university they were more cosmetic than deliberate. Hepburn accompanied his cuts with a vigorous defence of the economic status quo and the interests associated with it, especially in his determined resistance to the spread of American industrial unionism into the automobile factories of southern Ontario. Ontario applauded his efforts, for the most part, and so did the university, many of whose students enrolled as special constables at "Mitch's" behest in a famous strike at General Motors in Ottawa.

Economy meant that civil servants took a pay cut, and so did professors. Martin's salary descended from $5500 to $5060.42 in 1933-4, Flenley and Underhill from $4700 to $4445.84, all the way down to the "sessional lecturer" Richard M. Saunders, the most recent appointment (in 1931), who fell from $2100 to $1985.20.[45]

The cuts must be offset against the deflation of the period. The cost of living fell, and a salaried person was likely much better off even with cuts than he or she would have been in some notional continuation of the 1920s. On balance the members of the Department of History did not do badly. By 1938 Martin was back up to $5500 in dollars that had more purchasing power than they had in 1929. Saunders, low man when the cuts were first made and still a sessional lecturer, had surpassed his initial salary from 1931 and reached $2350. Better still, he was no longer quite at the bottom of the scale. (Below him, in 1938, were Miss M. MacLaren and R.G. Riddell, whose salary derived from his position in the Victoria College residence.) Faculty, especially junior faculty, made ends meet by taking on extra duties, such as teaching university extension: in 1933-4 Donald Creighton earned $520 from that source to supplement his salary of $2396.77; that year all faculty except Martin found ways of securing more money from the university besides their regular teaching duties.

Individual members of the department also earned money outside. Toronto was the centre of English-speaking Canada's cultural industries: publishing and, after about 1930, radio too. The publishers fed off general sales, but textbooks for the school system were their staples. Ontario and the other provinces maintained centralized curricula with prescribed texts, approved by the departments of education. Sales could sometimes be very large. W.S. Wallace's *A New History of Great Britain and Canada* is estimated to have sold 120,000 copies in its twenty-five-year lifespan and eighteen editions, but that was dwarfed by his *A First Book of Canadian History*, which sold 520,000 in sixteen editions between 1928 and 1944. George Brown was the all-time champion: his *Building the Canadian Nation* sold 600,000 over time; a later collaborative effort sold 730,000.[46] In the 1930s radio came along; younger members like George Glazebrook (hired in 1925 after the usual Toronto-Oxford progression) found this particular media a useful source, supplementing, in Glazebrook's case, general histories of transportation and external affairs.

There was also the *Canadian Historical Review*, run by Wallace down to 1930 and by Brown thereafter. The aim in this period was to maintain high scholarly standards without sacrificing the interest of the "general reader," a being presumably defined by the standards of the Historical Club or the other intelligent undergraduates the department yearly dispatched into the world.[47] It was not difficult to influence contributions towards these standards: most of the contributors in the interwar years either came from the department or taught there.

If individual budgets encouraged diversity and creativity, the department's own accounts were not quite as gloomy as might have been imagined. The bottom was reached in 1933 and thereafter things improved. Taken overall, the history department's budget expanded steadily during the later 1930s. From $29,450 in 1933-4 (faculty only are counted) it rose steadily to $32,071 in 1935-6, $35,500 in 1937-8, peaking at just over $39,000 between 1939 and 1942. Surprisingly, the 1930s saw an actual increase in the department's staff complement. Richard A. (Dick) Preston, a bluff Yorkshireman, came in 1937-8, and then departed for the duration of the war, and a medievalist, Bertie Wilkinson, came the next year. Wilkinson was considerably senior to Preston, and commanded the rank of full professor, with proportionate pay.

During the late 1930s and the first years of the Second World War some part of the budget must have become a casualty of inflation, but rigorous price and wage control kept inflation relatively low as late as 1945, when the budget reached $42,342 – this time including Miss Hahn, who received in the latter year $1000 for nine months. The wage was low, especially considering length of service and qualifications, but it was sadly compatible with remuneration for female secretaries in that era.[48]

As we have seen, Miss Hahn overcame her miserable pay to offer a personal touch to the department. It was small, which helped. Richard Saunders remembered it as close-knit and homelike. That was entirely natural in a group that could easily assemble around a single table and that held its meetings at its head's own home, in the evening. Miss Hahn did the typing and made the tea, but she also welcomed, provided continuity, and, on occasion, necessary advice. A department consisting, during this period, almost entirely of males needed the help. The great social occasion of the day was afternoon tea at Baldwin House "in a big room facing west"; it soon became a ritual. Mutual contact did not end with the teaching day, however. There was extension teaching, but beyond that there was the Historical Club, for which faculty advisers were assigned, and beyond that again a round of dinner parties, family parties, and friendly relations.[49]

Not all relations were friendly. It was well known that Donald Creighton and Frank Underhill did not get along, an awkward fact because they worked in the same area. "Donald disliked Frank's politics right down to the ground," Saunders recalled. "They avoided each other as much as possible." But it was not always possible in a small department with shared teaching responsibilities. That made it even worse. "I'm afraid Donald felt competitive with anyone teaching Canadian history," Saunders recollected.[50]

The change in regime with Martin's arrival coincided with an exercise in self-contemplation. The department's offerings in the 1920s had tended strongly towards Great Britain and the empire: on the honours side, there was North America and Canada under British Rule (History 1a), British History 1485-1688 (History 2e), the Constitutional History of England to 1603 (History 2f), British History 1689-1815 (History 3d), the Constitutional History of England since 1603 (History 3e), Great Britain and the Empire since 1815 (History 4e), a total of six courses. The United States after independence got one or two, depending on a student's choice of options; and Canada was represented under courses on the empire and in a fourth-year course on constitutional history. Europe, it must be admitted, was adequately covered, but, apart from the British Empire, no non-European part of the world was taught.[51]

Back in December 1928 the department commissioned Frank Underhill to try his hand at a revision of the history curriculum. After a considerable lapse of time, Underhill was ready, and in November 1929 the department gathered to consider what it must do. The report before it naturally reflected the views of its author, which were pronounced if not entirely consistent.

Underhill was a product of the University of Toronto and Oxford. Towards the latter he showed a flickering regard all his life, but, as one of his colleagues recollected, "Frank's was as pure a Canadian point of view as you could get." Being Canadian meant jettisoning the trappings of empire and adapting to life in North America. It was not surprising that in his report Underhill criticized the lack of North American history in the history syllabus. The course was drafted back in the colonial period when North American history was "regarded as beneath the notice of a gentleman." What was taught, especially in third and fourth years, had "very little relation to the life which students naturally entered after graduation." Instead, there should be a natural progression from remote past to immediate circumstances. Constitutional history was too prominent and insufficiently related to economic and social backgrounds. The tutorial group system had been applied too mechanically and divided and distracted the attention of students: the result, Underhill claimed, was "superficial work."[52]

Underhill's solution was in fact rather traditional. It emphasized chronology, moving from the Middle Ages in first year through to the world (Britain, the United States, and Canada) since 1783 in fourth year. George Brown proposed a different scheme, geographically divided, that would have students studying Europe, Britain, and North America in successive years, with separate courses on Canada and Europe since 1815 in fourth year. Ironically, Underhill's proposal embodied more British content than did Brown's, which led to Brown's idea being rejected. Finally, after a second meeting, Edgar McInnis and George Glazebrook advanced a plan that would divide pass from honours in first and fourth years, and combine the two in second and third years.

For all that, the curriculum changed slowly. By 1932-3 a course in Medieval and Renaissance Europe was in place in first year (History 1b); that course was to endure virtually unchanged until the 1960s. British and Colonial History – and Canadian – was taught in second year. The "English-Speaking World" was given in third year, along with the History of Cromwellian England; finally, in fourth year the History of Europe since 1815 and the History of Canada since 1763 appeared in the calendar. British history was somewhat reduced, but remained prominent.[53]

All this is of interest in showing what the department thought it should be doing. Yet its discussions, after all, only affected the course in Modern History. That still meant a small number of students.

If what was taught was important, who was taught was equally so. Class composition and class size, and the distribution of students in the honour and pass courses, were crucial to the department's functioning. It is useful to remember that the Department of History was far from an autonomous entity, and that it shared its students and its course requirements with other university departments. And history, though an important part of the university, did not have the largest honour "course." Its importance lay in itself – in the conviction that history, and especially Canadian history, embodied a national duty as well as a contribution to Canadians' definition of themselves. Secondarily, history's importance derived from the services it provided to other courses. The 800 or more students it taught in the honours program did not for the most part enrol in Modern History.

Quite the contrary. A survey of student enrolments in the early 1930s shows English and History as the largest course with a history identifier in its title. Modern History was much smaller – less than half the size. In some years, candidates in Modern History were measured in single digits: five in fourth year in 1932, for example. Philosophy (English or History option) was smaller still. Students in straight history comforted themselves with the notion that they were more serious, more committed, than their counterparts elsewhere. The fact remained that there were not very many of them.

The main reason for the strong student preference for English and History was not hard to find. It lay across Queen's Park in the provincial Department of Education, which in its wisdom prescribed history and English as ideally matched and mated courses for future high school teachers. By the 1930s the provincial government was having second thoughts on the subject. So, for that matter, was the English department.

The Department of History professed itself encouraged by this development. "The establishment of a specialist's teaching certificate in Modern History provides one obvious career for students interested in this subject," the department intoned in 1930, "and in forming the course the needs of the future teacher of history have been borne in mind." (The department, and the university, paid very close attention to what the province wanted to see in its high school teachers, and university courses were closely examined to ensure that they conformed to the government's expectations.)[54]

Of course Modern History was good preparation for "public life... the professions of theology, law and journalism, and the diplomatic and other civil services of the Dominion." The department did not reflect that it was its *teachers*, rather than its students, who had carved their niche in diplomacy. Other graduates had located in libraries, archives, museums, and, the department added, "in social work of various kinds." That also was true, but a fuller explanation would dwell on social work's utility as a destination for former female faculty like Helen Bott or Margaret Wrong.[55]

The result of these various shifts was a curricular earthquake of considerably more importance, as far as students were concerned, than the history department's ruminations on the shape of history. English and History was wound up, replaced between 1936 and 1939 by a new course in English alone.

History, cut adrift, moved to quite a different side of the curriculum. On its other, social science side, history had long shared a common first year with economics. That was now abolished, and in its place, largely at the instance of the Department of Political Economy, the university established a common first year for social science subjects, styled Social and Philosophical Studies, which would serve as common background for students in such subjects as political science, history, and sociology.[56]

In the aftermath, the Modern History course tended to increase so that for the first time, in terms of numbers of students, the Department of History was responsible for its own large clientele. The historians' decisions as to curriculum would by that token carry more weight in the future.

Yet it was just at that point that history faced its most serious controversy, one that would reach into Queen's Park and, eventually, into the office of Prime Minister Mackenzie King. The centre of the controversy, naturally, was Frank Underhill.

Frank Underhill's formal contest with the Canadian state began when he helped found the Co-operative Commonwealth Federation in 1932. The CCF proposed to solve Canada's economic depression by abolishing as much as it could of the capitalist system, and in the process it expended considerable time, effort, and oratory in attacking its enemies among the privileged.

The privileged were not, most of them, especially pleased. The spectre of the masses tearing down the classes, of socialism or bolshevism in Canada, was a fearful one. Nor was the distinction readily made between democratic socialism of the CCF variety and true bolshevism, Red in tooth and claw. These fears took their toll on political life, especially in a conservative decade.

The 1930s have tended to be remembered as radical. There were certainly plenty of radicals around, but the fact remains that there were always far more Liberal or Conservative voters than there were supporters of the CCF. A 1930s radical worked, and lived, in a conservative context, in which governments showed little sympathy for those who were trying to undermine society in difficult times, using the Depression to demonstrate the contradictions and inherent weaknesses of capitalism.

Ontario's government was especially unsympathetic to radicals and radicalism. Mitchell F. Hepburn, the Liberal premier, stood on the right of his party. Born a poor boy in Elgin County, "Mitch" had little sympathy for Toronto or Toronto's elites. Nor was he especially respectful of the autonomy of the university, which, after all, was paid for with public funds. Intellectuals also got short shrift from the premier: his education had stopped with high school, and he preferred the company of ostentatiously self-made men untainted by the pampering universities conferred on their graduates.

Mitch was prone to attacks of political excitement whenever he saw, or believed he saw, subversion of Ontario's and Canada's British heritage. He called and won a provincial election in 1937 on the issue of the invasion of Canada by the American industrial unions (the CIO). As war approached he turned his guns on the federal government, and especially its leader, Prime Minister King, for their sad lack of preparation for war. Mitch might be a Liberal but, as he told the world, he was no longer "a Mackenzie King Liberal." Not for Hepburn the doubts and hesitations of a national government concerned to keep the country together in the face of approaching war. The subtleties of dealing with Quebec were beyond Hepburn; the idea that history could be a healing force, and that Canada should indeed be kept together, was something he left to school textbooks and the Toronto professors who wrote them.

As war approached, Underhill was in the forefront of the opposition. The only result of the previous war, he claimed, was to bury 60,000 Canadians in the soil of Europe. Such bloodletting was too high a price to pay. Canada should, instead, seize its North American destiny and stay out of Britain's conflicts.

None of Underhill's colleagues was surprised at such sentiments. Underhill proposed them at department meetings and tried to get them embodied in the curriculum. Few of the colleagues thought as he did and some, Bertie Wilkinson especially, rallied round the British flag as crisis followed crisis in 1938 and 1939. So did most Ontarians and, indeed, most Canadians. Even the CCF wobbled and, in September 1939, supported war when King and his Liberals brought Canada into the conflict.

The reasons why Canada entered the war are much debated. Historians are divided between those who argue that Canada heeded the call of empire and rallied to its British heritage and those who believe that larger perceptions of the national interest were afoot. Certainly the spirit of solidarity with Britain was strong, and, when it became identified with the war effort, it had overwhelming force.

The University of Toronto reflected Ontario society in its hesitations during the 1930s. There were faculty, as there were students, who supported the root and branch reformation of the Canadian body politic. The students were more easily forgiven than the faculty. As prominent members of the community, faculty pronouncements were thought to carry weight. When Underhill or other faculty orated against capitalism, Canadian participation in some future British war, or some other established institution, their words were recorded and broadcast, sometimes by the newspapers or the radio, and sometimes by the police.

In 1935 President Cody received on his desk a communication from

General McBrien, commissioner of the RCMP, informing him that Underhill and another professor had appeared and spoken in unseemly company. No great harm had been done, apparently, but the president obviously should be informed.[57] And, it seemed, should be kept informed.

Cody was placed in a dilemma. His instincts and connections lay with those who complained about Underhill and who obviously wished him to do something. As a university president, and as one who could easily remember when the universities had indeed been the plaything of politicians, he understood that he had to respond, somehow, to political and public opinion. Yet as president it was also his task to reflect and represent his institution. Its inmates would not like to be reminded that it was the province that paid the budget and therefore called the tune in Toronto. Some of them believed the exact opposite should obtain. For Cody, the problem was the equivalent of squaring the circle. How could it be done?

Playing for time and awaiting events were the obvious first steps for the president to take. Cody allowed his correspondents to offer him their sympathy at having to deal with such a person as Underhill. When, in 1937, Underhill transgressed what conservative opinion considered proper behaviour, one young lawyer wrote the president that he was right to say nothing: Underhill was not worth getting upset over.[58] In any case, nothing Underhill said reflected directly on the university, for which he did not claim to speak.

Cody was nevertheless unnerved. Underhill had it in his power to undermine the university budget, annoy the Board of Governors, and enrage the premier. It did Underhill no good to hold his tongue; his past words – for example, that Canada had no interest in the poppies of Flanders fields – could be and were held against him, as they were in the spring of 1939. The opposition leader, George Drew, bellowed defiance at this un-British gasconade. In response, the premier and his supporters were threatening to cut off funds, and the margin for error seemed to be narrowing.

It was true that the traditions of British free speech and fair play protected Underhill. As Professor Frank Beare wrote to Cody, while "anti-British utterances as are credited to these men" – Underhill and Trinity College's George Grube – it would be entirely counter-productive to censor them in any way. "It seems to me," Beare continued, "that you have an exceptional opportunity to assert the necessity of independence for the University." Hepburn's threats to cut university funds were utterly irresponsible. "The way to meet people like Grube and Underhill is certainly not with threats and pressure, but with counter-argument."[59]

The Department of History was at first a bewildered bystander in the growing controversy over Underhill's right to say unpopular things on issues unconnected with his university duties. As Cody grew more nervous and impatient, as peace turned to war in the spring and summer of 1939, the president began to press Chester Martin to rein in his unruly subordinate. Martin agreed that Underhill was sometimes difficult and that his utterances could be aggravating. His comments on foreign and imperial affairs Martin himself found juvenile, "indefensible and unworthy of a scholar in Mr. Underhill's position."[60] Despite that, Martin urged moderation – meaning, in effect, support for Underhill's right to keep his job.

The president called Underhill on the carpet the following Tuesday. The history professor was "a trouble-maker who was costing the University untold sums of money (this business came just in the midst of trouble about our estimates)." Under the circumstances, Underhill was to explain, apologize, and promise to mend his ways – all this in writing. Underhill did as he was asked, and in his letter cited his distinguished war record as evidence of his innate patriotism. Meanwhile Martin, Harold Innis, Kennedy, and Samuel Beatty, dean of the Faculty of Arts, lobbied support for Underhill.

Cody was reassured. His political position had improved immeasurably through the expression of Underhill's contrition and the appearance of faculty support. His own conservative connections did no harm. When the Board of Governors debated the issue, the president easily rebuffed all attempts to go farther on Underhill. The issue was closed.[61]

Naturally, given Underhill's predispositions and the poisonous climate of Ontario politics, it was only closed temporarily. Underhill had become a very public figure, whose words were attentively read by his many critics for signs of backsliding. In August 1940 Underhill and the media met again, when he told a public affairs forum at Couchiching, among other things, that "we can no longer put all our eggs in the British basket." In the month of the Ogdensburg Agreement on hemispheric defence between Canada and the United States, and in the wake of the defeat of Britain and France on the continent of Europe, this was no surprising conclusion.

To Ontario's loyalists, it amounted to abandoning Britain in its hour of need. Illusion was as important as reality, and the hope of British victory was crucial. The attacks began again. Cody reacted predictably, and the faculty, with a good rehearsal under their belts two years earlier, took their accustomed position. This time the provincial government had the lead. Duncan McArthur, the minister of education, a man once considered for a post in the Toronto history department, asked the attorney general to investigate. Underhill's house was placed under surveillance, whether for Nazi, communist, or American agents we shall never know.

The incident naturally came up before the Board of Governors, where it was duly investigated and committees struck. Underhill's job was again on the line. Fortunately he had a good lawyer, a prominent Conservative who detested Hepburn. His colleagues rallied, and Martin once again took up the cudgels. "One of the best things about Martin was that he stood [consistently] behind Frank," Richard Saunders recalled.[62]

For a while things looked bleak. There were rumblings about the university's estimates from Queen's Park. Cody became even more nervous. It might be better if Underhill were dismissed, and in December Cody surrendered to those who wished to be rid of Underhill. Underhill's colleagues, especially Martin, Brown, Wilkinson, and Flenley, rallied. So did other faculty members, and Cody learned to his evident surprise that Underhill had wide support around the university. That delayed matters as the president pondered representations and petitions from faculty and students. Underhill was also resourceful in his own defence. He had friends in government in Ottawa, where Mackenzie King was still in power. King and Hepburn were at odds, but pressure, friendly or unfriendly, could still be applied. King's staff, which included a former history professor from Manitoba named Jack Pickersgill, applied it.[63] Ministers less antagonized than King concerning Hepburn phoned their friends in Toronto, and their friends included, oddly enough, the premier. Hepburn was persuaded that Ontario would suffer a black eye in public opinion if he allowed somebody to be persecuted for uttering what were effectively pro-American remarks. Canada's relations with the United States would be damaged. And think of the American tourists!

These mundane considerations helped clear Hepburn's mind as to the proper course of action. He denied he had ever considered punishing the university for keeping Underhill. (He made the denial to Carlton McNaught, a prominent Toronto publicist and a former member of the Historical Club.) The Board of Governors tried one more time, in June 1941, to get rid of Underhill. A motion to that effect actually passed, but was effectively vetoed by Cody. The incident was over, and so were the Underhill wars. Exhausted by the incessant controversy, and with his health affected, Underhill took the view that it might be wiser in the future to let others do the battling.[64]

The rest of the war was uneventful. Canada mounted a massive war effort and fielded a million men and women in uniform out of a population of just over twelve million. Taxes rose, drastically. Provincial budgets were frozen. The national government increased its role and its capacity as university graduates flowed into its ranks, where men like Mike Pearson and Hume Wrong were becoming increasingly prominent. Pearson by 1945 was ambassador to the United States, and Wrong associate undersecretary for external affairs. Vincent Massey was already high commissioner to Great Britain, and was spoken of as the next chancellor his alma mater, the University of Toronto.

As in the First World War, male and female students left for the front. Few of the professors were young enough to join the armed forces – a reflection of the hiring patterns of the 1930s – but some were called to war service. George Brown found he could expand his courses of lectures to include German prisoners of war at a camp in Oshawa. Glazebrook went to External Affairs in Ottawa, along with R.G. Riddell.

There were some replacements. The most unusual was the famous British medievalist, G.C. Coulton, who was translated from Cambridge at the age of eighty-two. He came at the instigation of President Cody, as a war refugee, and Cody gave him a place, and a small salary ($1500), as a special lecturer in history. Coulton took up residence at 74 St George Street, near Baldwin House. Though by title a lecturer, he gave few lectures; his work consisted of a few tutorial groups, which he duly segregated into male and female sections. "From the first," his daughter later wrote:

Father was accepted by the University as a visiting genius and treated with the reverent understanding due to such. All the same, at 82 he had a hard row to hoe. Increasing deafness would have made teaching difficult in any case, but he had, in addition, to cope with an almost-foreign accent and a wholly foreign idiom. He also had to get used to the idea that the college young of Canada are far younger, in everything but sophistication, than their fellows in England. For the first time in his life he was a little scared of his students, bewildered by their quick speech, their strangeness, their astonishing air of knowing everything that ever needs to be known.[65]

What the undergraduates made of Coulton, we do not know.

Enrolment dipped during the war, but only by 10 per cent. Unlike during the First World War, the Historical Club continued to meet. Though a number of temporary professors flowed through the department, it remained remarkably stable between 1939 and 1945. The real decisions that would affect the department, and the university, were being taken in Ottawa, as the government pondered what to do about the veterans. They had not been a force for order and stability after the first war; the trick was to keep them happy after the second.

The history department had changed very little, and very much, between 1924, when it moved to Baldwin House, and 1945. Its enrolments were relatively constant, and so was its staff complement. It was still an Oxford outpost but, unlike the period after the First World War, the faculty were mainly Canadian-born and graduates of Toronto itself, before they went on to Oxford for training and finishing. Thus Toronto's history faculty, rather like English Canada in general, was taking on an overwhelmingly Canadian coloration, though with a British veneer.

The Historical Club played a certain role in this development, as it had done in the 1900s. It provided a link between the university and society (with a large S), and identified and encouraged promising individuals – Maurice Careless, Gerald Craig, Ken McNaught, and Harold Nelson were four from the late 1930s – though for a future that was as yet unknown.

The department was more autonomous in 1945 than it had been twenty years earlier. Falconer had taken an intelligent interest in the department's affairs, though mainly on the administrative side. His plans to supplement Oxford with an American-scientific training bore partial fruit in the hiring of a couple of American PhDs – Brown and Saunders, with Saunders actually being an American. Falconer's, and the board's, cheese-paring policies set strict limits on what could be done; but despite cuts, the faculty managed to live and supplement its income, though at a cost in time and effort that would stagger today's professoriate.

The most striking characteristic of the Department of History in the interwar years was its social solidarity and its unity of purpose. Conflicts did exist, naturally. Underhill and Creighton notoriously failed to get along; other quarrels and disputations spontaneously occurred. Martin handled them imperturbably, less openly than George Wrong had done, but without seriously diminishing the sense of collegial responsibility.

Graduate work remained something of a sideline. There were plenty of MAS, and therefore plenty of students for graduate seminars, but the local MA degree had little importance inside the university. (It had plenty outside, where it conferred distinction and higher salaries in the teaching population.) There were only eleven PhDs conferred between 1925 and 1945, all in modern history. (The first in medieval came in 1949.) No Toronto PhDs were hired permanently at their own university, though some like Talman held very junior and temporary positions. The centre of life was, and continued to be, the undergraduate program and, within that, the honours course.

The department started to grow during the 1930s, but only hit its stride when the English department abolished English and History. As English expected, many students moved over into the new English Language and Literature course (always called EL&L) or, slightly later, into Modern History and Modern Languages (MHML) when that was established. But many also took the track towards the social sciences, and it was as a social science department, bracketed with political science, psychology, and economics, that history faced the 1940s and an incoming student generation that was intensely interested in the possibilities of a social science training.

Social science training, in turn, met the sense of possibility in Canada in 1945. History as taught at the University of Toronto had always self-consciously underpinned Canada's self-definition. That did not mean "mere" Canadian history, which, as we have seen, was taught in the setting of larger historical trends, whether imperial or North American. The experience of the Depression fashioned an agenda for the country that would be followed after the war. Political impotence, federal-provincial wrangling, and a sense of futility convinced many intellectuals that the older patterns of Canadian politics must be discarded. Not everyone went as far as Underhill into socialism – though socialism was something Underhill would soon retreat from.

In the University of Toronto's Department of History the predominant political coloration was liberal and Liberal – friends to Mackenzie King and his Ottawa government rather than to Mitch Hepburn and his raffish Ontario Liberals. It helped that before and during the war so many Toronto faculty departed for the civil service, or had friends who had done so: Pearson and Wrong in the 1920s, and Glazebrook and Riddell in the 1940s.

An exception to these developments must be made for Donald Creighton. A tory by temperament, Creighton was not so much at odds with the larger society than he was with his colleagues in the history department. A sense of being a minority (even if not particularly beleaguered) contributed to Creighton's sense of isolation.

The experience reinforced a conviction that Canada's needs must be addressed in a national, central fashion rather than in a parochial and provincial framework. Centralism also ensured that a united Canada would have a strong voice abroad; if domestic political attitudes derived from the Depression, views on foreign policy grew out of the war. Fundamentally, Toronto's historians bore a message of optimism: optimism about Canada, and optimism about its national potential. The fact that Canada came through the war without disaster, and with its national institutions intact and undivided by conflict, strengthened the message of conciliation and compromise that Toronto historians preached in their textbooks. Canada had not only a destiny increasingly separate and distinct from that of Britain and the British Empire, but it had a viable national itinerary to follow. That was the conclusion that veterans like Underhill had drawn after the First World War; many more drew it after the Second World War. The University of Toronto's Department of History was, under the circumstances, anxious to meet the challenge.

In the summer of 1945 the veterans were already steaming back across the Atlantic. The university nervously awaited their coming.

CHAPTER FOUR

Affluence

A MILLION VETERANS flooded back into Canadian life between 1944 and 1946. If their prospects were to be judged by previous experience, their long-term future would not be particularly bright. In the short term, there was re-establishment, personal or professional, and higher education was a recognized part of the process. The University of Toronto, and other Canadian universities, braced themselves, and, within the university, its Department of History drew in its breath. Perhaps it was only to be expected that the veterans would choose history as a means of explaining their personal past and the country's future; but perhaps not.

Certainly some things needed explaining. The world the veterans had left when they went into the army (or air force or navy) was a world of limitations: a place where jobs were scarce and opportunity scarcer, and where insecurity and doubt cast a shadow over society. The war changed that, but, many thought, only for the duration. The war emergency revolutionized Canada's industry, expanded its tax system, and turned its constitution upside down. Ottawa, not the provinces, was in the driver's seat. It was now a world where the old limits were being questioned, where qualifications and merit, not custom, counted. On the individual level, it was a world where a university degree was the passport to success.

It was a situation not much to the liking of George Drew, Ontario's

Conservative premier since 1943, when the discredited Liberals were swept out of office. Drew disliked experts, opposed centralization, battled Ottawa, and cherished the glories of the British Empire, which had just survived yet another challenge to its authority and solidity. Unfortunately for Drew, it had not survived unscathed. Britain and British values had triumphed and would have an Indian summer in Canada in the 1940s and 1950s; but they no longer had the power they once did.

The key to Canadian politics and political discourse after 1945 was the search for a better way of ordering society, so as to avoid the uncertainties and insecurities of the 1930s. George Drew's party sensed the mood and stressed change and progress in its election manifesto in 1943. But its triumph was only partial. Hampered by a hidebound civil service, and by a political philosophy that was after all conservative, Drew did not quite catch the national imagination, at least not enough to defeat his real rivals, the federal government of Mackenzie King and his Liberal party. The government in Ottawa, having led the war effort, also had the initiative for shaping peace, and took it.

Having taken the initiative, it enjoyed good luck as well as good management. The Canadian economy boomed in the late 1940s and early 1950s, effectively eliminating unemployment as a problem and contributing to an accelerating rise in living standards. With occasional dips and detours (especially in 1949-50), the prosperity thus begun lasted until the 1980s. The veterans were its chief beneficiaries, and their large families were the most notable product. A large part of the process, however, dealt with education: more, higher, and further than ever before in Canadian history.

The first step was to manage the veterans. They had been badly treated after the First World War, a fact that had political significance with a million Canadians in uniform in the Second World War. Mackenzie King therefore promised, and enacted, a veterans' package that included university tuition and a subsistence allowance for those who attended, based on length of military service. For those who needed it – and the married ones certainly did – the government made housing, often abandoned barracks, available.   It also offered to discharge early those veterans eligible for university entrance.

The effect was startling. Canadian universities boasted 21,869 undergraduates in 1920. The number was 35,132 in 1944, a quarter of them women. Full-time faculty totalled 4503. In 1945-6 Canadian universities enrolled 38,776 undergraduates, but in 1946-7 they had 61,861 and in 1947-8, 79,346. Emergency measures were taken to hire part-time or temporary faculty, all paid for out of the federal purse via the Department of Veterans' Affairs.

"I enrolled in Modern History and Modern Languages at UC," Fred Thorpe, a veteran, wrote in 1990. "I lived at home in Toronto, getting an allowance of $60 a month in addition to tuition and medical and dental care."[1] Thousands followed the same path or, if married, eked out a more modest but still feasible existence.

At the University of Toronto a whole new campus was established in a disused munitions complex at Ajax, to the east of the city. The older faculty, many of them veterans of the First World War, braced themselves. Administrators cast around for teachers to hire even if the future, after the veterans, remained inscrutable. The veterans, when they came, entered the honour courses in some numbers, and history in particular. Despite expectations on the part of some social scientists that the "vets" would choose their part of the curriculum, many picked history, raising the Modern History course to a high of seventy-three in the graduating class of 1949. Fortunately not all veterans were students. Some vets were available, and qualified, to teach, thanks to the classes graduated between 1937 and 1941. If the senior professors in the University of Toronto's Department of History were too old to go off to war, many of their graduates from the 1930s were not. Canadians were available, and qualified by reason of their PhD work;

and the department by and large hired Canadians.

The late 1930s produced talented classes and bright graduates, but graduates whose careers took a new turn. This is clear in comparing Lionel Gelber (Historical Club 1930-1) with Maurice Careless (Historical Club 1939-40), Gerald Craig (Historical Club 1938-9), Harold Nelson (Historical Club 1940-1), and Ken McNaught (Historical Club 1940-1). Gelber, who was independently wealthy, went to Oxford and to Balliol. He wrote books and, during the war (1941-3), taught briefly in the history department while championing a variety of international causes. The others emerged from the department a decade later. During the war all performed some kind of war service, Nelson and Careless in Ottawa, and Craig and McNaught in the army. But they had also already passed into graduate school, and the pattern they established was quite different from the one their predecessors had followed.

Careless did not go to Balliol, but to Harvard. Money was easier that way, as it was for other Toronto graduates. Craig went to Minnesota, and Nelson, eventually, went to Columbia. All took PhDs, and on the American model that had so horrified George Wrong twenty years before. Whether that "American model" actually existed is another question, and whether the University of Toronto's own conception of PhD work, established in the 1930s, greatly varied from the American standard is open to doubt. The important thing is that the Oxford-Balliol connection had lapsed by the end of the 1930s and the effect of the war, even with hundreds of thousands of Canadians stationed in Great Britain, had not reinforced it. "The doctorate qualification was taken for granted after 1946," J.B. Conacher drily commented. Only three permanent appointments of non-PhDs or non-PhD candidates (an important qualification) were made thereafter: Michael Powicke in 1947, Elliott Rose, who instead published a book, in 1955, and J.L. Cranmer-Byng in 1964.[2]

It was clear in 1945-6 that the old department that had survived the war would not be able to cope with the peace. The bulge in enrolment took a while to work itself through the system, year by year, and the bulge was concentrated in just a couple of years. Glazebrook and Preston, who had taken leave for the duration, returned from the wars, but that was not enough. Gerry Riddell toyed with the idea, encouraged by George Brown, but eventually decided to stay in Ottawa with the Department of External Affairs.[3]

Charles Stacey, who went from Princeton into the Canadian army as its principal historian, also gave thought to returning to Toronto. Like Riddell, he had an opportunity to stay on in Ottawa, as a lieutenant-colonel and head of the army's historical section. The pay was good, indeed very good, the staff large, and the responsibilities considerable. The pay was close to the top of the full professor range, and the department did not offer that. So Stacey stayed in Ottawa.[4]

The ranks of the full professors were gradually increasing. Donald Creighton made it in 1946, after two highly successful books in Canadian history and eighteen years of teaching. George Glazebrook was next, in 1947, and Edgar McInnis, who had also become a strong publisher (his series on the Second World War had sold well and received deserved acclaim inside and outside Canada), in 1950. Whatever their publications and distinctions, they were expected to do what they could in handling the veterans.

Creighton in 1945-6 taught tutorials in British and colonial history, Monday at 11, Tuesday at 10, Thursday at 9, and Tuesday at 2. He also taught a seminar in federal relations, Wednesday at 10 (Ken McNaught got 79, a mid-A, the highest in the class). And he filled up the week with tutorials in European history, Tuesday at 9 and Thursday at 10. At an average of ten students per tutorial, this was roughly seventy students. With the exception of federal relations (what would now be called federal-provincial relations), in which he had done work for a royal commission, none of these was anywhere near his official specialty.[5]

In 1946 McNaught was appointed "part-time instructor" and thrown into the breach; with him went an assortment of junior and senior graduate students, four in all, and two new lecturers, W.R. (Roger) Graham and Maurice Careless. The next year Jim Conacher, who had served under Stacey in the army, G.C. Patterson, Michael Powicke, J.M.S. Reid, and David Spring joined the staff. (Spring did not expect the appointment: "They'll never appoint me," he explained to Conacher, "I'm Jewish.") Later, George Bennett, a DPhil from Oxford, and Arthur Turner, a smooth and sophisticated Scot, joined. There were, as well, a number of women appointed, Misses Wright, Macdonald, and Albright. Of this list, Powicke, an Englishman who had taken his MA degree at Oxford, Bennett, and Turner were not Canadian; but of the British appointments only Powicke stayed.

This was not a bad record, comparatively speaking. History did much better in terms of permanent appointments than political economy, its rival and sometime twin. And that, in turn, may be a comment on Chester Martin's influence and effectiveness in the university.

Other appointments passed on, particularly the women. It was not an age of equality of treatment or of equal pay for equal work. Women appear to have been paid less than men (the records are insufficient to be certain in every case). Academic salaries were no longer protected by wage and price control, and prices soared in the years after the war. The lowest real faculty salary (instructors perched uncomfortably under the faculty) in 1950-1 was a woman's, $400 under her closest male colleague at $2400. Miss Hahn, the secretary, was paid less: $1400 for nine months. That might seem like an improvement over her wartime salary of $1000, but in reality it was not. Inflation had so eaten up ordinary incomes that $2000 in 1950 was equivalent to $1176 in 1939. The floor for full professors, $5500, equated to $3235; as Ian Drummond has suggested, that was worse than salaries in the 1880s in terms of purchasing power. A university committee recommended drastic salary increases, which were reluctantly put into place in 1951, despite a certain reluctance by the provincial government to face up to the problem.[6] The real surprises are not how many were attracted to the academic career, but how many, in difficult economic circumstances, remained.

Badly paid or not, they seem to have done the job. The bare statistics of students enrolled and students graduated give some idea of the magnitude of the task. It should be remembered that the task was accomplished by "jacks of all trades," instructors or tutors who by virtue of their appointment were considered ready and willing (and presumably able) to teach anything on the history curriculum. Maurice Careless, for example, tutored in History 1b, Medieval and Renaissance History from 476 to the Treaty of Westphalia, grading essays on Mohammed, St Louis, and Martin Luther.

"I don't remember a great deal about the lectures," Fred Thorpe wrote, "except I believe they were held in Vic chapel and we kept fit running between there and lectures in UC in French and Spanish. Bertie [Wilkinson] went on and on at one point about the Merovingians and Carolingians: he seemed to consider the names entertaining – I recall Chilperic and Gunther. 'Squeaky' Preston (so called by the students because of his English tenor delivery) once had at least a whole row of seminarians and nuns from St. Mike's walk out on him because he rather dwelt on the alleged iniquities of the Borgia popes ... Dick Saunders thundered at us from his pulpit (a Nonconformist chapel suited him perfectly); he was extremely effective and we thought he was first-class."[7]

Second year meant, for students in Modern History and Modern Languages (MHML), a choice. Thorpe selected two out of the three honour courses offered: Europe, 1648-1815 (Saunders and Glazebrook), and British and Colonial, 1485-1763, featuring Creighton and Preston. "The degree of ignorance of the sophomores of that day was such that some of us did not realize Creighton was a specialist in Canadian history! His lectures on British history were quite set-piece, some of us thought – even dull. Obviously a task he had to carry out, perhaps with little enthusiasm." In third year, "Chester Martin read lectures that were suspiciously close to [his book] Empire and Commonwealth and was succeeded by Donald Creighton ... who read lectures that were more than suspiciously close to Dominion of the North. In fact, once I got wise to that fact, I stopped taking notes in a loose-leaf notebook, as was my wont, and simply annotated D of N in the margin. There wasn't a hell of a lot of annotating to be done." Martin and Creighton had to compete with squeaking laboratory animals in the basement of the disused church that was all the university could find for its veterans.[8]

Thorpe wrote three essays in Canadian history for his tutor, Creighton. His most serious error in an essay on the Liberal-Conservative party, he remembered, "was that I had not given enough credit to the guy Creighton had not yet written the biography of, a chap who had done it all single-handedly."

"American history was better and started a rapport with Edgar McInnis ... I enjoyed working with him and he had a way of getting work out of some of us. In 4th year I could take one special option and chose International Relations, 1919-1939 with McInnis." The special option was a seminar, highly prized by the faculty as a sign of seniority; as a fourth-year lecture course Thorpe took Flenley's Europe since 1815, remembered chiefly for Flenley's habit of scratching his left shin with his right heel, and his right shin with his left: the Folies Bergères was its student nickname.[9]

It was not a bad system, even taking its follies into account. "We got excellent training from the department in those days," Thorpe considered. "Perhaps the paper credentials of the faculty were less impressive than today's, but they must be judged in relation to the times. A Canadian degree followed by one from Oxford or a PhD from Harvard, Columbia or Chicago provided a reasonable combination of qualifications which, in conjunction with the tutorial system, turned out a pretty good history graduate, by and large." It was a view widely shared.

The class of 1951 was the last to experience Baldwin House. In the spring, just after classes, the department packed up and moved north, under Dick Saunders's direction, to Sir Joseph Flavelle's mansion at the corner of Queen's Park and Hoskin Avenue. Senior faculty naturally got the best rooms, and with better views than at Baldwin House, where the grounds had been savaged to meet the requirements of an expanding engineering faculty and where the spacious southerly view of College Street was a thing of the past. There were more trees up around Flavelle House and a rather more recent building. As in Baldwin House, however, junior faculty found themselves sharing old bedrooms, with wallboard down the middle, in a row on the second floor. Again there was a constant clatter of students inside and outside offices and classrooms. The worst accommodated had to make do with space four feet square, up under the eaves.

In one respect the department did better than before. It appropriated for its tearoom Flavelle's panelled basement billiard room, and in these gracious surroundings socialization continued, every afternoon, for the next decade around a departmental samovar whose origins were, and remain, a matter of dispute. They were "old-fashioned but civil affairs," according to Bill Nelson, who spent a year in the department in 1952-3, and they contributed to the department's unity of purpose.[10]

At the top of the department (actually on the ground floor of Flavelle House) Chester Martin continued his reign, assisted by the senior committee of full professors inherited from his predecessor, G.M. Smith. Some liked him, and some did not. He was "a precious granny type," according to one junior colleague, with "anglo manners" and "a tendency to whistle when he spoke." His kind of history struck his juniors by the 1940s as fearfully limited, "so dry, so narrow in his constitutional focus." But he still had authority, an authority that may have irritated, but which also prevailed even when he was dealing with the irreverent. "He was on my PhD examining board," a student remembered, "and he fixed me with his glittering eye. I was sweating."[11]

The department's organization was, as these remarks might indicate, formal and hierarchical, governed at the centre by a senior group of full professors (the senior committee) under the head. It was in other senses highly flexible. Lectures tended to be given by long-time staff with experience in a given lecture course. By the standards of the 1990s they were not specialists in the field, except by experience in teaching it. There was, for example, no modern British specialist until Conacher, but the subject was taught nevertheless. The assumption was made that a basic qualification as a historian presupposed an ability to swat up, and then teach, in a wide range of fields, though it must be stressed that in 1946 the department's curriculum centred almost exclusively around the North Atlantic and in political history. "What did I know of Tudor-Stuart in 1946?" Jim Conacher lamented. He had taken "nothing since second year." He had the summer of 1946 to prepare two lecture courses and four tutorials, and he managed.[12]

Tutorials were even more eclectic than lectures. Creighton, a Canadian specialist working in British and European history, did not complain. The task was made easier by the nature of scholarship in the period. Divisions in history were not easily accepted. Though every historian undoubtedly had a preference for one or another area of the subject, that was something to be worked on and up in the summer. History's essential coherence was accepted, and with it conceptions of interchangeable, commonly held standards. It was generally possible to consume a great deal of the English-language material in, say, French or German history and still carry on teaching Canadian or British. And scholarship changed slowly, so that texts decades old could still be relied on. Given the department's traditional close attention to original texts and documents, obsolescence was even further retarded. Even in the 1950s and early 1960s it was possible to assume that two or three books, plus the documents, were sufficient to "do" Germany in the eighteenth century.

A glance at student essays gives a sense of the history taught – and required. Handwritten, creased down the middle, with bibliography on the outside fold, essays were expected to cover the "basics" and then proceed to argumentation, all in 3000 words, one each term in each course. One such paper, seven pages long, presented in Michael Powicke's tutorial in first-year medieval history, dealt with Louis ix of France. The bibliography, three books, consisted of general texts. While that might be accounted a minus by the standards of the 1990s, the presentation – without grammatical errors or syntactical horrors – might be sufficient to send today's professor into nostalgic fits. "In marking essays," according to Jim Conacher, "one always took grammar into account."[13] That was less of a burden in the 1940s and 1950s than in the 1970s and 1980s, he added. The argument in this particular essay, though scattered, was not unreasonable for a first-year student. The grade on the paper was 71, a mid-B.

Another student, working for Donald Creighton in a third-year tutorial, found he had used two primary sources and six secondary works for one essay, and three books and four articles for another. "Creighton expected analysis," he wrote, and praised what he termed "careful and thorough work on the authorities."[14]

Grading standards were not easy. First-class honours were rare in the 1930s and 1940s. Grading Toronto essays was different from what he had been used to, Conacher recalled. "I thought a lot about standards, and I worked closely on this with Careless and Spring." Coming from Queen's, and trained there by a tiny department of four in the 1930s, Conacher could not be sure what had to be done. Careless and Spring, both products of the Toronto system, had a clear idea, and

Conacher followed their advice. Adopting Toronto was less a matter of accepting direction than acculturating oneself to a strong and pre-existing academic society.

Lectures in the medieval course started with the decline of the Roman Empire and subdivided among military anarchy, economic disorders, state socialism and rigid control, and spiritual factors. Spiritual factors naturally led to a consideration of Christianity, its vicissitudes and its triumph in the fourth century. The next lecture dealt with the barbarian invasions, and successive lectures proceeded chronologically.

Canadian history, in second year, was even more traditional in form but not entirely so in content. No history existed before the French. "The voyageurs were spirited, enterprising, always fond of the country," and, later, "spirited, enterprising and happy." Staples appeared with the voyageurs, and with the fur staple, economic history. But not only economic history was treated: demography received a nod, with immigration and settlement. The national period got optimistic treatment, with the lecturer (George Brown) empha-sizing "a pan-Canadian approach rather than petty parochial politics." The federal government ("the Dominion") commanded the support of a generation of professors, whether conservative like Creighton or liberal like Underhill, Brown, or McDougall. Few if any of their colleagues would have disagreed. That said, discussion of recent federal-provincial relations was muted in the history course of the late 1940s, and limited to a factual summary of issues and events.

The department did not directly impose any particular point of view. Lectures were effectively optional, especially towards the end of the year. They were even more optional in the pass course, where standards were lower and admission easier. In Canadian history, Creighton's *Dominion of the North* was recommended, but so was Arthur Lower's *Colony to Nation*, identified in a student's notes as "conservative approach" and "radical approach," respectively. On New France,

Parkman was still on the list, as he had been since Sir Daniel Wilson. Perhaps that was because the available literature on Canada was so scanty that every possible book, polemical, amateur, or not, had to be included, from W.C.R. Wood's *The Passing of New France* to Wilfrid Eggleston's *Road to Nationhood*, a study of recent federal-provincial relations.

Later years demanded more from the students both in knowledge and in essays, but the limitations of the library precluded detailed research. In comments, it was analysis rather than particular books that graders concentrated on. It is difficult to generalize from small samples, but it seems that essays were shorter, and the specialized expectations of the grader less. Students, however, were assumed to have, and probably did have, a broader background in both history and English composition when they came to university. That had been true in the 1910s, 1920s, and 1930s. Conacher remembered that students did not necessarily know more history when they arrived in the 1940s.[15] General skills they had, but as to history, "I used to believe that it didn't hurt if students hadn't had any history before: we could drill chronology into them here." Students coming from Ontario's grade 13 at least had the background from Flenley's text on *Modern Europe*; and Flenley's prosperity, like that of other senior members of the department with their texts, was much increased thereby.[16]

Term work, including tutorial performance, term tests (if any), and essays, counted for one-third of a student's final grade. Two-thirds depended on the final examination in the spring. It was always possible to recoup a dismal year by a final burst of energy and enthusiasm – and sufficient knowledge. The rhythm of the school year varied accordingly: leisurely in the fall, gradually picking up steam in the winter, climaxing in the last weeks of April or the first week of May.

The veterans were mixed with ordinary students but, being older and, on the whole, more assertive, they gave a tone to the period. "The students in '46 were very impressive," Conacher recalled. "They were my contemporaries." They included Doug Fisher, a future MP and newspaper columnist, Sid Wise, a future dean at Carleton, and T.B. Miller: "Doug was particularly formidable." There were women veterans too, particularly Jean Houston and Jean (Jamie) Jamieson, "both about my age."[17]

The bulge, to judge by enrolments, lasted from 1945 to 1951 or 1952, with the peak of 8846 in 1947-8. Thereafter, numbers dropped steadily, until by 1952-3 they were reflecting the baby "bust" of the 1930s, when couples had prudently postponed or cancelled their plans for family formation. That year there were a mere 2800 student enrolments in history classes; the next year there were only 2676. But while they were at the university, the vets cast a long shadow.

Underhill was understandably popular with such an audience. "In terms of lecturing and grabbing students, he was a blaze of light and excitement and involvement," Ken McNaught remembered. "Evidently Underhill spoke more extemporaneously and more provocatively than Creighton," a student of the time later reflected, "and was something of a spellbnder in his own staccato way." His reputation for humanity was more advanced than Creighton's, though the two men were rated about equal in fairness among the undergraduates.[18] As a PhD supervisor Underhill was less satisfactory: there was not enough direction or attention.[19]

One other development affected enrolment and teaching. In 1951 the university did away with the four-year general course. Thereafter students in arts and science divided into only two streams: general BAS or BScs, graduating in three years, and honours BAS, who took the whole four years. Some critics thought the change represented a further devaluation of the general arts program, but their complaint was definitely in the minority. If general arts had to be modified or even partly sacrificed to keep the honours program going, that was a price worth paying; and the Department of History was especially willing to pay.

Teaching in general courses, such as History 1a, was largely allocated to junior faculty. In the early 1960s, Maurice Careless tried to interpret the system to a junior appointment just arrived from Great Britain. Referring to lectures in History 1a, Careless candidly explained "they must be very general and they will be given from hand to mouth, so to speak. Certainly, there are very few lecturers – especially new men in the course – who are ever more than half a lecture ahead in preparation as the year goes on!"[20]

As in the years before the war, faculty duties did not end with the classroom. The Historical Club continued to exist, with faculty advisers attached. There were more history students to choose among than in the 1930s, given the inflation in size of the Modern History course. Their extracurricular interests were met by founding a Modern History Club and, for the first time, a Graduate History Club.[21] A new generation of hosts accommodated the Historical Club: Sidney Hermant, a keen member of the club in the 1930s; Roland Michener, the Conservative MP for St Paul's (and later governor general); Sidney Smith, president of the university; Canon Cody, now the chancellor; Colonel Eric Phillips, chairman of the Board of Governors; and Moffatt Woodside, the Victoria College registrar and future dean of arts for the university. "The fact of contact with these hosts was incidental," Jim Conacher later argued. "What was important was to get the brightest students involved."[22] Whether or not that was the case was frequently debated inside the department, but, like so many other issues, such discussions were kept strictly away from the ears of the membership and the hosts. In the early 1950s the Historical Club remained an important part of the department – but a part whose function and performance were beginning to be called into question.

Social life was closely organized, and new arrivals were immediately integrated into a pre-existng social pattern. Satuday nights were reserved for entertainment, dinner parties at the homes of the senior professors. Juniors were invited, and expected. Such functions varied in tone: German white wine at the Creightons and soft drinks at the Browns, who were strict teetotallers, at least when Mrs Brown was present. (Brown was reputed to have sipped sherry on occasion.) There were alternatives to dinner at home, though not in a university setting. The Faculty Union, ensconced in Hart House, does not seem to have exercised much drawing power on history faculty. Creighton's diary records an endless series of dinners and lunches at the Chez Paree on Bloor Street or the Fifth Avenue restaurant, and cocktails at the roof bar at the Park Plaza Hotel. An evening out, including drinks, dinner, and taxi, cost $15 in 1953.[23]

Nor was socializing strictly confined inside the faculty. A party at the Carelesses in the spring of 1953 included the publisher John Gray and the CBC personality Tommy Tweed as well as the Creightons and the Spencers.[24] Gray published both Creighton and Careless; and the CBC was more than an occasional source of interest, and income, for Toronto faculty. It was a reminder that there were advantages to life in Toronto, the centre of English-language publishing and broadcasting. The history department was a national institution in part because it coexisted, and even cohabited, with other national institutions.

Toronto's advantage could be exaggerated, and was in the eyes of some of its members. Creighton complained that his department was regularly ignored in the distribution of fellowships in the Royal Society of Canada, a view that surprised his friend W.L. Morton at the University of Manitoba. "One tends to assume out here that senior men in central Canada will be looked after," Morton wrote, "which is sometimes mistaken and can be ungracious."[25] Perhaps the discretion characteristic of the period can be assigned part of the blame.

Faculty politics were also closely held, inside the faculty circle and within the norms of discretion. Outside and elsewhere prudence prevailed. "The only things I ever heard Underhill say about Creighton he said in public," McNaught continued. On the other side, "Creighton never held my close association with Underhill against me."[26] The two men met at parties and sat through daily teas for, literally, decades.

Creighton later denied there had ever been a feud between him and Underhill and stated that it was a concoction of a sensation-hungry media. In the sense of avoiding public rows, Creighton was right, but at bottom there was a gnawing resentment. Creighton could be quite explicit about Underhill: he complained about Underhill's easy ascent to a full professorship. It wasn't hard to be a radical and denounce capitalism on a full professor's salary, he would grumble. He did not need to add, though he did, that he, Creighton, had not had as high a salary as Underhill, or for as long.[27] It may also have been the scorn of the researcher for the non-researcher, or of the publisher of books for one who failed to publish, except political ephemera. It may have been the dislike of a conservative for a liberal or radical, and a growing distaste for the easy liberal explanations and justifications of Canadian history. It probably was all of these, and with a personal element added.

There was, however, more to the story than that. High-strung and temperamental, Creighton was not universally beloved among his colleagues. The senior ones disliked him, but he did not do much to ingratiate himself with younger ones – people like Jack Saywell, who in the 1950s was the rising star of the department.[28] Creighton, for his part, felt neglected. "Nobody ever tells me anything," he exclaimed in 1953 on being introduced to a new colleague, an American. That Creighton did not much like Americans was well enough known; but within limits he was prepared to tolerate them. Some might even be mistaken for Canadians.[29] The feeling of grievance increased as he gained in historical stature outside the university with the publication of his text, *Dominion of the North*. Though there was strain, there was no open break or public disruption, and that gave the later Martin years a tranquillity that would afterwards be remembered.

Chester Martin passed his sixty-fifth birthday in July 1947. He did not retire that year, or the next, or indeed until July 1953, after twenty-four years as department head.

Martin was the second and last head of the Department of History. His departure coincided with another: the death of Harold Innis, head of the Department of Political Economy, late in 1952.

These events gave President Sidney Smith the opportunity to implement an idea that had been around since the days of Sir Robert Falconer: to change the headships, permanent and powerful, into chairmanships, on the American model that so many faculty by then found familiar.

The incoming chairman of political economy, Vincent Bladen, accepted the change in title on being assured that Smith did not mean anything by it. There is no record of what historians thought of the change; they seem to have accepted it without any serious demur.

What Smith intended by the change is obscure, but it seems altogether likely that he wished to diminish the head's authority. The easiest way to do that was to make the headship rotational, and thereby to clip its powers.[30] Heads were appointed without term, while chairmen could be had for a limited number of years. Heads were preeminent, in scholarship and prestige, over their fellows, and chairmen need not be. The beneficiaries of such a move would presumably be the other members of the departments concerned, but by breaking down the authority of the head Smith was trying to alter, and not slightly, the balance between the academic departments and the administration of the university. He was definitely not altering it to the departments' advantage.[31]

In 1952-3 these matters lay in the future and in the realm of theory. Historians are generally reluctant to engage on such terrain, but that did not mean they would not find occasion to contemplate other matters. In 1952 that meant the issue of personality.

There were a number of personalities in the history department who might have been considered suitable material for the chairmanship.

Underhill, next to Flenley in seniority, would be almost too old to be chairman when his turn came, though age had been no bar to Martin continuing. George Brown seems not to have been considered a possibility. He was fully engaged by work for the University of Toronto Press, which in those days existed in an industrial outhouse just behind the history department. Edgar McInnis was a successful publisher, duly promoted to full professor. He and Creighton received recognition of a kind when the Board of Governors approved leaves at half pay for the next year, 1951-2 – an unusual step that would become considerably more common in the future. But McInnis abruptly resigned in February 1952. Sidney Smith mourned the loss, for which he could not find an explanation: "Nary a word from him, except his curtly worded resignation!"[32]

Donald Creighton turned fifty in 1952. At the height of his powers, and perhaps anticipating the extremely favourable reception his biography of Sir John A. Macdonald would receive, Creighton believed that the headship of history would be a proper recognition of his achievements. He was startled and depressed, therefore, to be interviewed by Sidney Smith and told why he would not get it. There would be a chairman, like G.M. Smith in the 1920s, and not a head, like Martin. The job would go instead to the last holdover from the Wrong years, Ralph Flenley, his senior, and a full professor since 1927.

"Had a long talk with the President this morning," Creighton wrote on 9 September 1952. "Without disclaiming responsibility for not having made me head of the Dept. he suggested that he did not believe that my colleagues would have accepted me in that position." Creighton blamed George Brown, with whom he was certainly unpopular, and George Glazebrook for this development, a bad sign for the future. (Glazebrook, who had taken an appointment on the security side of the government in Ottawa at the end of 1948, must have acted at long distance.) For the present he could do nothing but accept the situation, and the consolation prize of an appointment to chair a division of the graduate school.[33]

That year the departmental budget was fixed at $106,200. The faculty complement was twenty, with provision made for instructors and readers, and, of course, Miss Hahn. Some things did not change: the departmental tea continued to be made. But some things did: as chairman, Flenley ran the department in close consultation with a senior committee. In March 1954, for example, the committee met to distribute scholarships and then to consider appointments. Creighton, who attended, wrote that "Wilkinson very annoyed that [a junior faculty member] is now certain to stay another year, though we voted in favour of dismissing him on previous occasion in February."[34]

Salaries in 1954 ranged from $8200 at the top down to $3225 for a slot for a special lecturer, unnamed, to replace George Brown, on leave for the year. Wages in this period moved upward in a stately progression, in small annual increments. They were calibrated according to rank, and sometimes when promotions were slow – they were very slow – the financial consequences could be severe for the individuals concerned. The hierarchy and protocol governing personnel were by this point more complex than they once had been. The chairman spoke to the dean of arts, in this period Samuel Beatty, who made recommendations to the president, Sidney Smith. The president in turn took such matters onward, to the Board of Governors.

Leaves and promotions were in the hands of an economy-minded board, which was already facing drastic salary raises to compensate for the inflation of the late 1940s. Martin exerted himself to secure promotions for his faculty and expressed annoyance when they were not forthcoming. Jim Conacher and Michael Powicke were overdue for promotion, he told the dean. The dean was not unsympathetic. Writing to Sidney Smith in May 1951, he admitted that Martin had "a happy and efficient group of colleagues" and felt "it would be worth while to give him a hint that you would hope to be able to promote Conacher and Powicke next year." The year following, George

Bennett, Craig, Nelson, and Spencer could be advanced. McDougall, whose case Martin particularly favoured, continued to be held back by a shortage of funds. There *was* a way in which the shortage could be solved, Martin realized, but as he wrote, "I do not like to think that my own retirement is the only thing that can procure McDougall's well-merited promotion."[35]

Beatty's plan came too late to keep Bennett, who resigned in mid-year to take a post in Oxford as of January 1952. The offer was too good to refuse, Beatty explained to Smith, and, given Bennett's salary, that was not surprising. Martin had problems finding a successor — something that also did not surprise Sidney Smith.[36] When another historian, a virtually permanent associate professor, was offered the headship of the history department at McMaster, Smith himself improved the offer that kept him at Toronto. In the event the individual concerned went up by fully $1500, the largest single salary increase in the period.[37]

The next year, 1953, A.C. Turner, appointed only in 1952, resigned to become chairman of the Division of Social Sciences at the University of California, Riverside.[38] That same year another promising applicant withdrew his name from consideration so as to take a job at Williams College: Williams, he explained, had a "considerably higher" salary level and the cost of living in rural Massachusetts was considerably less.[39] This was discouraging news, though it does indicate that Toronto was competing for appointments at the same level, and at the same time, as good American schools. Those already on Toronto's faculty were evidently of sufficiently high quality to have an obvious market value, and in a market that in certain areas was continent-wide. If the comparison were made to the civil service, the results were even more discouraging. R.A. (Bert) MacKay, only eight years older than Creighton, and with a comparable academic career, was making double his salary as acting undersecretary for external affairs in Ottawa.[40] These examples served to remind the president that he lived in a competitive academic environment and that he could not always rely on inertia and loyalty to keep his staff.

The administration took no chances the next year, 1954. When one assistant professor received "an offer ... of a materially higher salary from another institution," Flenley urged immediate action. Given "our desire to keep him," Flenley wrote, "I suggest that he be granted an increase of $400, raising his salary to $5,300."[41] It was a reminder that the University of Toronto did not live in a world of its own, and that its budgetary stringencies could have undesirable consequences.

Not all personnel matters had a clear solution or a happy outcome. Martin saw David Spring, who worked in the department between 1946 and 1949, as the eventual successor of Frank Underhill in teaching modern British history. Spring had moved to Johns Hopkins, a better offer, and had written a book that was expected to make him top of his field. The department prepared an appropriate slot and negotiated Spring's reappointment two years in advance, only to see its schemes fall apart.[42]

Flenley was understood to be a transitional appointment, and the chair was his reward for long and genial service. He took leave of absence on 1 January 1955, at full pay, and retired to his native England. His successor, this time, was Donald Creighton.

Creighton learned his fate at lunch with Sidney Smith at the York Club. The president, he told his diary, had offered first a gin and tonic, and then "offered me the 'headship' (not chairmanship) of the Dept. of History, at the level of Woodhouse [English] and Anderson [Mathematics] ($8900-9000)."[43] Creighton was understandably exhilarated; but there is another version of the conversation. Smith told Vincent Bladen that Creighton held out for the headship, and asked Bladen, as chairman of political economy, to talk him around. "I urged him to accept the new title as long as it involved personal responsibility, not committee government," Bladen wrote. "The title, I argued, was unimportant; the nature of the appointment, vital. He agreed and the title of Head gradually disappeared from the Faculty of Arts."[44] Nevertheless, what Creighton got was not what he thought Smith had initially offered.

The two men did not discuss an alternative candidacy for the job, that of Frank Underhill. Underhill was sixty-four. If he became chairman, he would have to be carried on yearly contracts, or so it was said. Against that inconvenience, Underhill had some support among his peers, particularly McDougall and possibly Brown. Creighton, however, had none. There is no evidence that Smith ever considered Underhill's appointment, or that he sounded opinion in the department on the subject. Given Underhill's slight publication record, and Smith's regard for research and publication, his selection would have been unlikely in the best of circumstances.[45]

What happened next is fairly clear. Creighton was made chairman, not head, of the Department of History; and he was offered $8100, not $8900. He became acting chairman on 1 January 1955, when Flenley took leave, and full chairman on 1 July. Creighton was satisfied by the recognition, if not by the salary or the precise status. Smith would increase the salary for "professors of distinction" the very next year, which may have satisfied some of Creighton's complaints: his salary rose by $1000.

But the post as chairman did not prove to be a happy choice, either for Creighton or for Smith, or, needless to say, for Underhill, who took Creighton's appointment hard. As chairman, Creighton would be bound by the department's committee structure. A senior committee had existed under Martin and Flenley, and it would continue to exist. The chairman had to consult and, if possible, respect the opinions of his senior colleagues and contemporaries, the full professors. It was not an experience that either party would enjoy.

The department Creighton inherited contained fifteen full-time faculty, with a total budget, including unfilled posts, Miss Hahn and an unspecified secretarial assistant, and supplies, of $111,643, practically double what the department had cost as recently as 1945-6.

Little has been said about the experience of graduate students in the postwar period. In general, whether or not they had been Toronto undergraduates, they occupied a marginal place in the department's affections. There were graduate seminars and there were plenty of graduate degrees awarded, especially MAS; and between 1940 and 1960 there were fifteen PhDs too. These graduates were expected to seek their fortunes elsewhere.

The marginality of graduate education was a by-product of the honours system, which concentrated teaching attention and hours on the honours students. Undergraduates received an intensive education, but a "professional" formation, with its American connotations, was reserved for graduate work. "Students go from Political Science and Modern History into professions, business, the Civil Service and other employment," Donald Creighton wrote in 1954, "but whatever professional training is necessary must be secured after the degree in Arts is obtained."[46] Toronto was fulfilling an obvious function in producing its undergraduates – turning them into responsible citizens and even servants of an expansive and optimistc Canadian state. This was a purpose not far removed from George Wrong's original conception of the true function of history.

Graduate work was in Creighton's view something different. It had a purpose, then, but it was not a purpose that the Toronto history department unqualifiedly accepted. Graduate supervision was recognized on the worksheet, but with so few PhD candidates – seldom more than one or two a year – it did little to distract attention from the main task. That this was so made the University of Toronto's history department something of an oddity among major history schools in North America. The size of its staff certainly made Toronto a significant factor; and the propensity of other schools to raid its faculty suggests that the hiring of the late 1940s and early 1950s had produced a department that could and should be placed among the leaders in its field. But there were doubts. It was especially strong in Canadian history, and Canadian history had little resonance outside Canada. It had hired good people in British and European history, but they were young and had yet to make their mark. Others argued a more fundamental problem. As long as it maintained its traditional orientation to undergraduate teaching it could not even be a major school: that quality in the postwar world was measured in terms of graduate students rather than undergraduates.

Yet observers generally considered the quality of history at Toronto to be high. William Dray, a Canadian philosopher of history, argued that he had been inspired to try to redefine his discipline by his observation and appreciation of what the Toronto faculty did. Creighton read the book that embodied Dray's conclusions with pleasure and interest, and said so in a letter to Dray. Responding to Creighton, Dray noted that "the discussion [in his book] arose for me out of a tension between my intuitive conviction that history as it actually exists, and as I had seen it practised by my teachers at Toronto, is an intellectually respectable discipline, and my discovery that what the formal logicians, with great plausibility, have said about the necessary features of any rational enquiry, scarcely seems to apply to historical investigation at all. The problem, as I conceived it, was to bring theory somehow to terms with practice."[47]

The practice, at Toronto, was seldom to delve into theory, and then largely on the graduate level. Graduate seminars were usually small and generally concerned with practical rather than theoretical problems. Fred Thorpe, who took an MA in 1949-50, studied Europe 1870-1914 with Flenley and McInnis and four others. Flenley's historiography course, in contrast, was "enormous," if not particularly useful. (According to another student that year, it was "a complete disaster.")[48] The highlight of the year, however, was the Graduate History Club at Baldwin House, "where graduate students and faculty discussed research work in progress and chatted informally. Fledgling graduate students had the opportunity for the first time of listening to their professors cross swords," while balancing Donald McDougall's occasional shafts and compliments.

Not everyone was satisfied. Margaret Banks, who enrolled in the PhD program in 1949, hoped for a career in university teaching. She inspected Toronto before coming, discovering that in the faculty's view, "Well, that is fine, you can come and take your PhD if you want to, but, of course, you realize you won't be able to get a teaching job in the university because university history departments don't hire women." Banks refused to believe it. There were certainly women teaching history in Canada, she knew, and surely she could join their ranks. Only later did she discover that at least three of the four women came from well-established university families and that another, in political science, was the daughter of Malcolm Wallace, the principal of University College.[49]

Underhill, her supervisor, was charming and interesting, and his seminar on the Liberal tradition a great success. Underhill by 1950 was a mere shadow of his former radical self. As far as some of his students were concerned, he was well on his way back to the Liberal party, abandoning the CCF as an aberration. Banks's MA duly followed, and then her PhD, on Edward Blake, a favourite topic of Underhill's, and, he said, the subject of his future book — a book that would never appear.

Banks's thesis, on Blake's career as an Irish MP, was completed in 1953, and a book eventually published, but despite the success of her work there were no history jobs to follow. "I am sure I wrote letters to every university in Canada in 1952," she remembered, and the answer to every one of them was negative. She became an archivist and a librarian as well as a published historian; but for Banks, as presumably for other women, full-time history ended at the PhD.

The 1950s admittedly were not an easy time for those seeking faculty jobs. Writing in 1957 from his position as chairman, Creighton observed: "I think ... there is a slight superabundance of historians trained in Canadian and British Commonwealth history." Yet "I have a feeling that it will not be long before there is a really serious scramble for men. Already, almost all our students in every field have got jobs, or good prospects, ahead of them."[50]

That was not quite true. Even when students had jobs, they did not always keep them. One Creighton student found himself teaching at a small Baptist college at a minimal salary that he managed to supplement by minor admininstration. But when he was reported (by one of his students) as actually taking a drink at a local army base, his career as an administrator was finished. Shortly after he quit, throwing himself back on Creighton in hopes of another job somewhere, anywhere, else. Creighton's optimism about job prospects evaporated in the grim search that followed. Happily, the man eventually found satisfaction, and tenure, at an Ontario university, but it was not easy.

Appointments at Toronto did not cease, however. John Cairns, from Toronto via Cornell, was appointed in 1952; Willard Piepenburg, an American with a Cambridge PhD, that same year; Jack Saywell, a UBC graduate with a Harvard PhD, in 1954; and Morris Zaslow, a graduate student at Toronto itself, in 1952. (Zaslow's PhD, in 1957, was the first indigenous doctorate to be accepted as a qualification for appointment to the Department of History.) Ramsay Cook, another Toronto graduate student, was appointed in 1958. That year, 1958-9, the proposed estimates for the department reached $171,690, including $165,450 in academic salaries, $5600 for the two secretaries, and just over $1000 in supplies and maintenance. Twenty-two faculty were on the roster, and the deaprtment had hopes for another.

Universities and society in the 1950s were still working through the low birth rates of the Great Depression. The students of the 1950s, hard-working and conformist, resembled those of the prewar generation. Canadian society was experiencing a prolonged economic boom:

suburbs were spreading, highways building, and optimism and self-confident nationalism defined the public mood. Ontario did not alter so much as expand in this period; but as it expanded there were misgivings that its educational establishment was not quite what it should be. Sidney Smith, in his annual reports, drew attention to the deficiencies of the university, the deplorable state of its library, and the failure of the Ontario high school examination system to provide truly or even adequately educated undergraduates to the university.[51] What was on the surface a complacent and materialistic decade proved, on closer examination, to be afflicted by doubt, and by the desire for self-improvement. Institutions like the Historical Club, or like the Department of History itself, could remain outwardly unaltered; but inwardly the department and its club were beginning to cause concern.

Two particular factors seem to have been at play. The club represented a call, or a drain, on faculty time – as did the Graduate History Club and the Modern History Club. But the Historical Club was not restricted to history students, and in most years history students were not even a majority. Nor were members of the department entirely happy with the quality of the membership, or how the members conducted themselves at meetings. Some suggested admitting graduate students, but that idea was rejected as inappropriate. Others pointed out the obvious, that the exclusion of women reduced the pool of potential members and made it necessary to delve deep into the second-class range. In 1954 one professor lamented that his best candidate was devoid of humour and wit: "None of my other second year students qualify for consideration. *My good students are all women*, except for [student X]."[52]

In January 1955 Underhill, Careless, Conacher, and Willard Piepenburg, a recent appointment and the club's adviser, met with the club executive. There were real concerns, the students were told, concerns so serious that the department was beginning to question its connection to the institution.

"We proposed to them," Underhill wrote, "as a method of avoiding the abrupt cessation of the Club, that in future the Club membership should be limited to twenty undergraduates of whom at least twelve should be history students. We were agreed that it is better, if the Club continues, that it be a Club of limited membership and that it remain restricted to male undergraduates." The Historical Club executive "admitted the general truth of our criticisms of the quality of Club meetings in recent years." To remedy it, they agreed to accept whatever nominees the department put forward (these included Don Forster, a future appointee as president of the university). If even this drastic measure failed, the students were warned, the department would likely disassociate itself from the club.[53]

That would take more time, and another chairman. For the moment, the club carried on, and the department for its part turned its attention to other matters. Underhill departed for Ottawa, where he became writer-in-residence at Laurier House, Mackenzie King's former domicile, at a salary of $6600 per annum. Eventually he moved on to Carleton University as visiting professor of political science and spent there a happy retirement, surrounded by students and apparently contented with life.

The same could not be said of Creighton. Creighton was temperamentally dissatisfied with life, morose, touchy in his dealings with his colleagues, and given to fits of depression. His eminence and prominence in his profession, his active social life, and his devoted circle of friends never quite satisfied his desire for recognition. The result was that Creighton's talents, his hard work, and his marked good intentions often fell on barren ground, at least as far as the history department was concerned. That was so largely because of the friction his personality engendered.

"He had no sensitivity in dealing with individuals in the department," Jim Conacher remembered.[54] Not all individuals, to be sure, and not all the time. Some who feared Creighton's mordant view of life found his eye softened when it turned to them; even Americans in the department did not find they were condemned to outer darkness merely for that reason.

Creighton was least successful with his most senior colleagues. George Brown in particular resented Creighton and disapproved of his selection as chairman. When he got the news, he called three of the middle-ranking faculty, Jim Conacher, Maurice Careless, and Gerry Craig, to meet him on a weekend to discuss the crisis. Poor relations with Brown went back to the 1920s. Brown, like Underhill, had been senior to Creighton, and for years had earned more money; and it was believed Creighton felt indignant about that fact. He let it be known that he had no great regard for Brown's talents as a scholar, and word inevitably got back. Bertie Wilkinson also resented Creighton as chairman, a telling blow from someone regarded as the other academic star in the department. Wilkinson had no small reputation as a controversialist in his field, and some believed he applied the talent closer to home, as required. Saunders, the next most senior, was a friend of Brown's, though not directly antagonistic to Creighton.

The problem extended beyond administration. The Cold War was on, Canada was an ally of the United States, and Creighton disapproved. His colleagues found his comments on the subject difficult, if not worse. "It was more than tiresome, it was painful," Conacher reflected, and over time it placed a constraint on the exchange of opinion and even conversation in the department. In public, "he was constantly complaining of lack of recognition," which came hard to colleagues, less published and less recognized, who were expected to respond to the need.

Those same colleagues had the power to frustrate Creighton's plans, particularly in the realm of appointments. Appointments were very much the province of the senior committee. Without their support, Creighton could not appoint. In one case, when the chairman favoured a young Canadian historian then finishing an MA in the department, the senior committee blocked the choice.[55] That was not an isolated incident, and over time such episodes took their toll.

Finally Creighton took advantage of a year's leave and the Harold Innis professorship in 1959 to resign and decamp. In his place the university's new president, Claude Bissell, appointed Maurice Careless. With Careless's appointment, the postwar generation came into its own.

What kind of department did Careless inherit? It was, to begin with, still strongly Canadian by nationality, with an admixture of Americans and British. Toronto undergraduate degrees still predominated, though American graduate degrees were in the majority. All those hired for permanent positions in this period were men.

The hirings of the 1940s and 1950s had the effect of greatly strengthening the department's expertise in British and European history, while maintaining its strength in the Canadian area. Martin and Brown departed, but Saywell, Cook, and (in 1963) W.J. Eccles replaced them.

The honour program continued to be the centrepiece of the department's life. Canada was, it was believed, noted for its honour programs.[56] In Canada, Toronto's was pre-eminent. Nowhere else were there so many honour students, as compared with the general or pass variety. Nowhere else, the staff argued, were there as many good students.

Eccles, when he arrived from Alberta, had mixed feelings about the students and the honour course. It was a different magnitude, of course. At Alberta or Manitoba, where he had previously taught, excellent students were an occasional thing, almost a rarity to be treasured. But where there might be one at a smaller campus, there were ten or twelve at Toronto. That made a difference in teaching, Eccles believed.[57]

But not perhaps a sufficient difference. The honour system at

Toronto boasted first-, second-, and third-class honours. That was the Oxford way, but it seemed out of place in a setting where honours meant some kind of distinction. Third-class honours students were not very much better, if at all, than the pass or general course students. Yet they received a far better education, at least in terms of the resources poured into it. Perhaps a crude form of equality was at work, leavening the honour course with an average ingredient, but it left its mark in sleepy tutorials and ineffective discussion. In Eccles's recollection, the honours system in practice was not quite what George Wrong thought he had devised.

In the late 1950s or early 1960s the honours system was not really questioned. The great matter at issue, year in and year out, was how to feed it. The burden, in the department's view, should be equally shared. The criterion was the number of students whose work had to be graded. A certain allowance was made for graduate supervision, and it was understood that very senior members were to be allowed their pick of "special" seminars in fourth year. That, at least, was the assumption.

In practice, again, it was a little different. In March 1958 the department's undergraduate secretary, Harold Nelson, prepared estimates of enrolments in history courses for the following fall. History 1b, the entry course, would probably have 230 students. That meant twenty-five tutorial groups of nine or ten each, or twenty-five faculty hours, since all tutorials, even in first year, were given by full faculty members only. In 1958 the magic number for each member of the department was eighty-eight: eighty-eight students whose work had to be marked – multiples of essays and, eventually, exams. A thesis counted as ten exams, but theses were few and for most non-existent. George Brown, the most senior, had two theses going (or twenty points), and Brown did not have to participate in History 1b.

The number of grading assignments was only part of the story. There was also class time, in lectures, seminars, or tutorials. Creighton, as chairman, had six hours per week, one hour of lectures (half a year) in History 3d (Canadian), a tutorial group in the same course, a fourth-year seminar, and a graduate seminar. George Brown had eight, and Willard Piepenburg, one of the most junior members, ten and a third, including nine tutorials in two different courses.

In a stable demographic situation like that of the 1950s, such a system did not greatly strain the department's resources. But by the mid-1950s a different demographic picture was emerging. The birth rate had risen sharply at the end of the Second World War and it stayed high. The veterans had produced the baby boom, and, eventually, the youth generation. Hordes of teenagers, more than ever before and in higher proportion to the rest of the population than ever before, flooded the high schools. By 1958 there were more high schools, and more a-building. This was no blip like the veterans. Temporary stop-gap methods would not do. It was not difficult to foresee a problem for the universities, and for the University of Toronto.

On the grand scale, the provincial government met the problem by building new universities and expanding existing ones. Where there had been colleges, there were now universities. By 1968 Metropolitan Toronto had two universities spread over five campuses. York University was spun out of the University of Toronto, while Toronto itself acquired two satellite colleges, Erindale and Scarborough, each twenty miles from the downtown St George campus. Each campus hired historians, who duly became members of the Department of History.

But how to meet the problem on the smaller scale? What would happen to the University of Toronto's traditional methods of education under the pressure of numbers? Between 1945 and 1950 the Department of History solved the problem by hiring temporary staff and adding to its existing complement. Many of those added were still there, and still young. There was some flexibility in the system as it stood, but sooner or later the department, and the university, would have to make a choice. The department could go on hiring faculty, who were essentially tutors, to service its undergraduates. The honour requirement, that every honour student attend a faculty-led tutorial in every honours course, entailed nothing less. Such a development would necessarily be expensive, and the expense would be controversial. Few other departments employed tutorials in the same way as history. Where they existed, as in certain economics courses, they could be as large as twenty or thirty students, which made a mockery of the teacher-student contact that the tutorial system was supposed to encourage. The fact that tutorials as practised in history were a minority institution suggested that in a competition with other departments for necessary funds, history would find itself at a disadvantage, without strong support from the central administration. Of course, if times were flush, and they were, the evil day might be postponed. It was, however, altogether unlikely that it could be put off forever.

Not everyone in the department understood that this might be so. To them it was axiomatic that the university's integrity, its essence, and its character were identified with the honours program. The honour courses gave every student an identity, and made the student known, in the program that existed in the early 1960s, to at least three history faculty members in each year from second to fourth. Students tended to take the same courses, which gave them an opportunity to identify with their honour course, especially if it was Modern History and not a hybrid like Modern History and Modern Languages. Such identification came at the expense of the colleges, whose academic programs at this period were limited to the traditional "college subjects" of English, French, German, classics, Near Eastern studies, and ethics.

Course identity, and escape from the anonymity of a mass university in what was becoming the mega-city of Metropolitan Toronto, not to mention the mini-city of the university, were highly positive reinforcements for students. What affected students also touched faculty.

The marks meetings remained the centrepiece of the academic year. There was one meeting for each year – second, third and fourth – at which students' standings and futures were batted around, and where averages and grades were raised (seldom lowered). The tempering of justice with mercy most often occurred when faculty expectations and student performance diverged.[58] Obviously such things could happen only when the faculty reliably knew the students involved.

This they could do because of the high degree of concentration and prescription that the honour courses demanded. Concentration had two meanings, however. Students were concentrated in few courses, but courses were concentrated in few areas: North America, the Commonwealth, and Europe. That this was the case was, by the early 1960s, generally deplored,[59] and the department set out to remedy the situation. It did this by establishing and then reinforcing new areas of study in Russian, East Asian, East European, Latin American, and eventually African history. The idea was to allow students to follow a sequence in a given area through the last three years; at the same time the department snapped the link with classics by disestablishing Greek and Roman history as a compulsory field of study. Existing areas, such as Canadian and British, were also strengthened by the hiring of new faculty and, in some cases, by the return of old graduates, such as Ken McNaught, who returned to Toronto in 1959. C.P. Stacey, superannuated from the army, also returned that year for a part-time appointment teaching Canadian military history and foreign policy. In 1962 George Glazebrook reappeared from lengthy service at External Affairs. Both men somewhat offset Creighton at the senior level, though Glazebrook took little part in departmental society and administration.

Another link was snapped at the same time. The history department had for some time been impatient with the Historical Club and tried, in the mid-1950s, to reform it. To Careless, it seemed that the effort had not succeeded. Greatly to the annoyance of the alumni hosts of the club, he broke the formal link between the Department of History and its offspring, and sent it off into the world to fend for itself. (Careless himself, while chairman in the early 1960s, nevertheless acted as host to meetings.) The club survived very well under the circumstances, and in the late 1960s maintained a vigorous existence, the more so because it finally admitted female undergraduates to membership. In the 1970s it finally fell on evil days and dissolved. Subsequent efforts at resuscitation were unsuccessful.

The expansion of offerings necessitated an alteration of the curriculum, or that part of the curriculum the department controlled. It is clear from the context that what was intended was a reform only, to some degree a liberalization of procedures and a broadening of choice. Donald Creighton put it this way, in his diary: The curriculum committee met on 19 February 1962, "at which we found an acceptable core of required subjects, with a good deal of freedom of choice. However, one [probable?] result is the break-up of soc and phil first year, for we need two courses for our plan there."[60] That did not happen, but the new order passed anyway. As Creighton recorded on 16 March 1962, "The new curriculum adopted: Ken McNaught being opposed almost alone. Meeting over by 5.15 pm."[61]

The effect of the curricular reforms of 1962 was to dilute the principle of concentration. The extent and effect of the dilution were much debated both among liberals and conservatives in the department, with the effect that the reform achieved only a temporary appeasement of the forces that were seeking to alter the existing arrangements at the University of Toronto. When next the subject was raised, in 1966, the circumstances would be very different and, for the university, much less stable.

That this was so was the direct result of the demographic crisis that hit the universities of Canada in the mid-1960s. The governments of Canada, both provincial and federal, accepted that greater magnitudes of students must be taught, and released their grip on their budgets.

Both at the downtown campus and at the new satellite colleges of Scarborough and Erindale, new hiring was authorized, with effect as follows:

Year	Appointments	Departures
1961-2	6	-
1962-3	2	1
1963-4	5	1
1964-5	11	1
1965-6	5	1
1966-7	4	-
1967-8	9	1
1968-9	7	2
1969-70	10	3
1970-1	6	2
TOTAL	65	12

These figures tell only part of the story. In terms of age, the effect of the new hires was to tilt the department downward. The median age dropped, down to thirty-six. Moreover, the sheer numbers of those hired meant that "new" (since 1960) outnumbered "old." Relatively few of the newcomers were graduates of the University of Toronto, so that unlike the influx in the 1940s there was little institutional familiarity to be relied upon. Six of those hired before 1970 had Toronto PhDs granted between 1960 and 1969, however. Not many more of those appointed were Canadian by nationality, a reflection of the dearth of Canadian PhDs in specialized fields in the early 1960s. Although there were some British appointments, the bulk of the new appointments were American. As the reader might expect, the great majority of them were men. Ten women were hired between 1960 and 1969, of whom only four – Anna Cienciala, Ann Robson, Natalie Davis, and Jill Conway – were more than temporary. The point about these selections was less that they were American than that they were highly professionalized and highly specialized – and trained to be so as graduate students. There was no great difference between Canadian and American graduates in this regard; the University of Toronto's own graduate offerings were modelled on, and in fact closely resembled, those at familiar American universities. This situation was an ironic reprise of George Wrong's worst fears: and now the enemy, as he would have seen it, was within the gates.

A certain amount of confusion resulted. Not merely circumstances, but the times seemed out of joint. As student enrolment edged up, the department had recourse to graduate students as tutorial leaders – in exceptional cases, it told itself, but the breach of principle was there anyway. That was a relatively private matter, but there were other, more general phenomena that affected the life of the Department of History and to which it could not remain immune. Anti-Americanism was in flower in Canada in the mid to late 1960s, thanks to the Vietnam War and civil disruption in the United States. It was not hard to transfer resentment against the United States government to individual Americans and, in Canadian academia, this reaction was hardly uncommon. There were too many Americans, some argued; they were undermining Canadian traditions and turning Canadian campuses into local satellites of American culture. Canada, some nationalists believed, was under threat, its distinctive culture becoming submerged in a tide of American technology. *Lament for a Nation*, a 1965 book by the philosopher George Grant, harked back to a simpler time before American values came to dominate Canada – a process Grant considered well-nigh irreversible.

The debate at times became quite ferocious. Light gave way to heat, with American immigrants being blamed for a wide and indeed extraordinary range of academic and social evils. The extreme claims made by the most intense Canadian nationalists had the effect of discrediting many of their arguments and reducing their instinctive supporters to an embarrassed silence. Yet the phenomenon of a large influx of American academics, most of whom knew little about Canada, existed and formed a backdrop to the developments of the later 1960s.

One other occurrence affecting the character of the history department deserves to be mentioned. The department's physical surroundings changed again, and not favourably, in 1961. The university administration wanted Flavelle House for its own purposes, namely the shelter of the Faculty of Law. A new university building was being constructed on St George Street, to be named after the late Sidney Smith. Its tenants included everything from psychology to fine art, and a large lecture wing was attached on the south. The building itself was strikingly modern, with a California-style plaza back and front and large picture windows facing south towards Lake Ontario, which could actually be seen from the fifth or sixth floors. On the outside, Sidney Smith Hall was encased in grey concrete slabs; inside, cinder block walls, linoleum tiled floors, and glass partitions around the top of each office ensured that nowhere would there be total darkness. The offices had a certain crude hierarchy: large at the end of the long corridors, for chairmen and similar beings; then along the corridors there were outside offices with windows and space for a seminar table and chairs; and, finally, there were windowless inside offices for junior faculty, with space for a bookcase, a desk, and a chair. The furniture was gunmetal grey, with rubberized corners. And so history moved from the old and faded splendours of Flavelle House to the new and less certain ambience of the university's new complex.

At first there was considerable jockeying for position. Especially coveted were outside offices with south-facing windows. Their tenants duly moved in, apportioned their books along the shelves, and settled back to enjoy their new surroundings. The enjoyment lasted until the first sunny day. It was then discovered that the windows admitted large amounts of heat and that the ventilators beneath them could not hope to compensate. Worst, the university had not installed air conditioning – omitted, some said, in a last-minute economy move. In the corridors undergraduates shuffled from office to office or stared down at their professors from high banks of seats in cinder-block lecture theatres. Grim and stifling, Sidney Smith Hall (reduced to "SidSmith" by the undergraduates) did little that was positive for staff or student morale.

The physical surroundings could not be differentiated from social arrangements. In this category, too, the new building left something to be desired. Teatime at the history department survived the move, but not for long. Miss Hahn valiantly tried to carry on in one of the outside offices, but faculty trying to sip tea found themselves banging elbows and jostling cups in a facility unsuited for the purpose. Tea dwindled and then, in the mid 1960s, it died.

The demise of the departmental tea coincided with the departure of Miss Hahn, whose particular province it had been. The new departmental secretary, Bea Stafford, presided from an office just outside room 2074, which housed the junior secretaries in a pool in the middle, and then, at the south end, the chairman, Maurice Careless. On the north side, there was Donald Creighton. The associate chairman, R.A. Spencer in the mid-1960s, perched elsewhere, in a regulation office down the hall.

There was no longer sufficient space in the department's precincts (the east half of the second and third floors, plus a few scattered offices on the fifth) for the department to meet. When it gathered it had to migrate to common office space inside Sidney Smith or to other buildings that in the late 1960s were springing up almost daily to the north and south along St George Street. Contact was maintained over lunch at the Faculty Club, half a block behind Sidney Smith, where a regular contingent of historians led by Stacey occupied several tables every lunch hour to debate the issues of the day over beer and sausages and salad.

Departmental meetings were still extremely important − perhaps more important in the late 1960s than before or since. At issue between 1966 and 1970 was the shape of the department's teaching program and the fate of the honours course. Such sweeping changes were not intended at the begnning; on the contrary, change began with a relatively modest reforming document that proposed to take the 1962 reforms one step further and, by doing so, to do away with encumbrances and anachronisms.

These sentiments were most strikingly expressed by Bill Nelson, · who had taught briefly in the department in 1952-3 and again since 1962. In a memorandum to his colleagues in March 1966, Nelson suggested that the Modern History course as presently constituted had serious flaws. "It has neither the clarity and integrity of a narrow and rigid curriculum, nor the flexibility and openness of a permissive curriculum." It was unimaginative, featuring as it did three years of survey courses to students who in high school had presumably had their fill of such. The British and European core of the curriculum had been shattered by the 1962 reforms; all that remained was what Nelson termed "the sprawling survey course in Canadian history, decorated if not distinguished by the nationalist and extra-curricular rubric that makes it compulsory for Modern History students."

Nelson was careful to insist that he was not in favour of dismantling the existing tutorial system. Tutorials, however, were an expensive method of teaching, and the department was not getting full value for its money. Indeed, it could not even agree on the nature of the beast. Was a tutorial a quiz section or was it a mini-seminar?

In Nelson's view, the department should abandon compulsion and opt for freedom of choice. The old first-year course, medieval history, should be abolished and replaced by a course on historical methodology. In subsequent years, "with the teacher-student ratio now existing, there could be as much personal contact as now exists, but it would be based upon choice rather than conformity to an imposed curriculum ... In all classes, large and small, there could be a reasonable certainty that students were there because they wanted to be there."

Philosophically Nelson's proposals were in tune with the times. For some years students had been chafing at what they claimed were excessively rigid structures. Outside the university, compulsion and conformity had become bad words. Civil rights, freedom rides in the United States, national liberation abroad: these ideas resonated in society at large and it would have been surprising if they had not exercised an influence inside the university. The year 1966 was already the age of freedom; soon it would be the Age of Aquarius.

Nelson's colleagues responded cautiously. Gerald Craig, speaking for the department's curriculum committee, carefully set down the history of the honours course and laid out its traditonally recognized advantages. Students were regularly exposed to differing viewpoints in team-taught survey courses and to further differences in tutorials. Tutorials were the centrepiece of the Toronto system, and lectures were far less important than elsewhere. Because all faculty were expected to participate in tutorials, the result was a greater equality of treatment for all. "The tradition is that, with the exception of a few senior and distinguished professors, all members of the staff do approximately equal hours of teaching, with appropriate allowances made for departmental, Faculty or administrative responsibilities."

The sequence of courses was logical and coherent, and consistent with students' requirements. Compared with other North American universities, Toronto's system was unique, but also highly successful in terms of the placement of graduates in graduate schools and their ability to win fellowships, such as the coveted Woodrow Wilson award.

Craig obliquely admitted that there was a difference in treatment accorded to students in the honours program and in the general course. "All honour students are treated alike, that is, they are entitled to entry into the same courses and to receive instruction at the same level. The

General course is envisaged not as a receptacle for failed honour students, but rather as a self-contained course with somewhat lower standards for entrance and standing."[62]

Craig's memorandum was circulated and formed the basis of discussion at a department meeting at Massey College, the university's newly founded graduate college, on 29 March 1966. After an hour of general discussion, the meeting broke up into working groups, and then reconvened to consider what it must do. There was plainly a disposition for change, but as yet no clear idea as to what the change should be. At the same time a number of faculty were profoundly opposed to what they took to be radical alterations in the history honour course. Their wishes had to be considered and their views appeased, if possible. A subcommittee chaired by Craig, and with John Beattie, Bill Nelson, and Craig Brown participating, undertook to make recommendations. It was time for a pause, but it was not to be a pause that refreshed.

On 11 April Creighton recorded that over lunch with C.P. Stacey, P.C.T. White, and Ramsay Cook, "Stacey and White very alarmed at the prospect of calendar revision."[63] The professor most opposed, however, was Harold Nelson, a graduate of the department, a fact that by 1966 put him in a distinct minority. On the 14th, Creighton noted that "Harold Nelson has written a letter of passionate protest against contemplated changes in the history curriculum: and Maurice Careless fears a blow-up in the Dept. with possible resignations. Talked with him and with Ramsay Cook about the crisis."[64]

It is not now possible to reconstruct the swirl of rumour and gossip that surrounded the curricular debate. Some general conclusions are nevertheless obvious. In argument, the reformers prevailed. The demographics of the department – the predominance of youth and the newly hired – favoured their cause. Yet their cause would not have prevailed without support from some of the departmental establishment. In terms of personalities, Gerald Craig was key to what would follow. A Toronto graduate, a Canadian historian at least part of the time, active and influential in departmental affairs, his opinion had weight with the traditionally inclined. In March, Craig spoke for orthodoxy and tradition; but by April or May, after lengthy discussions in the curriculum subcommittee, he had apparently switched.[65]

That may have been what so greatly alarmed Creighton. Though Careless as chairman contemplated putting off the issue until the fall, events had assumed their own momentum. Creighton described what happened in his diary. On 16 May there was once again a "full meeting of the department at 2.00 PM. Gerald Craig introduced the new scheme: Bob McNeal, W.H. Nelson also spoke. Robert Spencer gave a long, detailed and very effective criticism of the plan. I also spoke, indicating my opposition. At about five o'clock, while the debate was still going on, I left."[66]

The meeting adjourned with no decision taken. Two days later, 18 May, a final meeting was held, where the final decision was to be made. Creighton again attended, coming into the city from his country residence in Brooklin. "Determined to go to Toronto by early train and make a final statement at the second curriculum meeting. Drafted a few headings for my remarks: planned to give an historical explanation of the present history curriculum. Meeting began at 9.30 a.m. Most members of the dept. declared themselves and Craig, W.H. Nelson, Spencer, and others also spoke again. I gave up my idea of an historical explanation but talked briefly but forcefully in support of the old curriculum. The vote was taken at last at 1.00 p.m. Twenty-five for the new plan: four – H. Nelson, Spencer, White and myself opposed. Had a drink and lunch with Spencer. Not too depressed by what has happened. I myself am now out of it: and will do no more to [aid?] or impede the danger."[67]

That fall the new curriculum finally took shape. The first-year course, History 1b, would be altered. A new course on Canadian history would be offered. There would be a substantial increase in the number of third-year courses, with a more varied teaching approach.

This latter would be achieved at the expense of fourth-year courses; fourth-year students would be reallocated to third-year courses, where a third of the places would be reserved for them.[68]

The new curriculum duly appeared in the fall of 1967, and for three years it was the standard for the history honours course. The honour course itself did not last much longer. It and every other honour course were abandoned by the university in response to student and faculty pressures at the end of the 1960s. The "elitism" of the honour courses and the manifestly unequal standing of the general course proved a liability, one that faculty and adminstration were no longer willing to bear. Historians and history students such as Bob Rae took a large part in the events that overturned the old system of teaching and university government. Their history lies outside the boundaries of this study, although the result does not: in June 1970 the University of Toronto graduated the last of its honour students, and the Modern History course, with its cousins Modern History and Modern Languages and the revivified English (History option), ceased to exist.

In many respects what occurred between 1967 and 1970 was a footnote to the history department's own crisis of conscience in 1966. The old system, so apparently strong and successful as late as the mid-1960s, had become top-heavy. Apparently elitist, the honour courses in fact admitted and taught many students whose abilities and performance were average or less than average, and who benefited little from the faculty time and contact lavished upon them. The difference between these students and the much less advantaged general arts students was not especially apparent. The demands that the honour courses made on faculty time were considerable, and faculty time was expensive.

The training that faculty had received was expensive too, in time, money, and personal commitment, and faculty had their own ideas as to how best to put that training to work. Specialization on the faculty level and voluntarism on the student level seemed to be the appropriate answer. Compulsory courses and a strictly prescribed curriculum, the essence of the honour courses, were not. The reforms of 1966, which all but eliminated compulsion and eroded the distinction between the honours and general courses, therefore struck at the heart of the honour system. The abolition of honours entirely a few years later was, under the circumstances, an afterthought.

The Department of History entered the 1970s greatly changed in role and self-definition. The loss of the honours course closed a long and honourable chapter, and it was unclear what would replace it. Yet history at the Univesity of Toronto was hardly without resources. It was bigger than ever before; its faculty were well-trained and productive; it had a wide capacity to teach subjects that spanned every continent; and it had successfully provided an alternative for the old European-centred historical universe in which most of its professoriate had grown up. Its students would certainly be affected by the demise of the honours couse, but it was difficult, in 1970, to predict how. The history department would have to deploy its resources to best advantage in a present-minded world where the purpose of history was by no means self-evident. History was sinking in popularity in the United States, and what happened south of the border exerted a powerful influence over Canada too. Inside the university there was an unfamiliar academic world where all the old principles of university government and faculty authority were coming under stress, if not under threat. It would be a taxing time.

CHAPTER FIVE

The Fullness of Time

I N 1967-8 THE DEPARTMENT OF HISTORY at the University of Toronto numbered forty-seven full-time faculty on the St George campus. The median age of the faculty that year was thirty-six, not a surprising figure considering how many of them were newly hired over the previous five years. Five years service marked a veteran in 1968 (56 per cent of the department had been hired since 1962).[1] Half of the faculty were thirty-six or younger, a fact not without significance in considering the willingness of the department to overturn its previous curriculum in 1966.

Of those on staff, 30 per cent had at least one Toronto degree, including 14 per cent whose PhD was home-based. Harvard, Oxford, Columbia, Berkeley, Cambridge, and London were next, followed by a scattering of doctorates from Cornell to Cracow. (Cracow, incidentally, was the only degree outside the British Isles or North America.)[2]

Twenty years later, the faculty's world was rather different from what it had been in 1970. For one thing there was less mobility, a consequence both of the shortage of university jobs in the intervening years and the aging of the professoriate. The composition of the Department of History was as a result remarkably stable. Of fifty-six full-time faculty on staff in 1990 on the St George and Erindale campuses, thirty-one had been in place in 1970. Of the full professors, only six had less than twenty years' service in the department.

Another consideration applied to the question of faculty mobility. In the late 1960s and through the 1970s there was considerable agitation over the nationality of faculty members. It was in an odd way a reminder of the political roots, and the taxation fertilizer, that anchored and sustained Canadian universities. The expansion of graduate education in the 1960s excited certain expectations among those who granted the money to pay for it, including the idea that in the future Canadians could be trained, at home, for home-grown positions in the expanding university system. It followed that those positions had to be available, when required. But when the demand came, new positions were exceedingly sparse: the boom of the 1960s in faculty appointments was definitely over.

There was, however, yet another complication. Some fervent Canadian nationalists worried that the American inflow of the 1960s had skewed the orientation of academic departments towards the United States. US-born or trained academics, they argued, would buy American, ignoring local traditions and slighting perfectly well-qualified Canadians. Toronto historians could easily recognize the argument and appreciate the emotions it aroused: "national" pre-conceptions, presumed or actual, were strongly present during the debate over the history curriculum in the mid-1960s. Some Toronto graduates, clutching their PhDs but unable to find academic jobs, were inclined to sympathize with this point of view. More broadly, it found an echo in national politics, especially in the nationalist wing of the Liberal party.

Government responded by altering immigration policy. The Liberal Trudeau government imposed a two-tier "search" system on universities that required universities to look in Canada first and to satisfy the immigration authorities that there were, truly, no suitable Canadian candidates. As a result, in areas where Canadian candidates were truly scarce, searches could be prolonged: in one case, up to two years.

Internal migration was theoretically easier. Payscales were crucial in this area, especially if prospective staff already had jobs. Toronto became a notoriously costly city, both by Canadian and international standards, even if it also liked to celebrate itself as a "city that works." That was true in many respects: after the 1970s Toronto's lifestyle did not suffer by comparison with Montreal's, and as Quebec became engulfed in linguistic and nationalist troubles many found its southwestern rival more attractive and less upsetting.

During the 1970s Toronto did not always fare well in terms of comparative pay: it was known that academics in the more prosperous western provinces were better paid; and in the late 1970s, when Quebec elected a separatist government largely staffed by academics, it was true there as well. That government lost its referendum on sovereignty-association in 1980 and shortly thereafter discovered new priorities, which included an across-the-board pay cut to professors and other public servants. This had the effect of removing one of Quebec's comparative advantages in the academic field, although it made little dent in other, equally significant, areas.

That this was so was a matter of considerable regret in the history department. Ramsay Cook and W.J. Eccles both made a strong impact during the 1960s, the one as an analyst of French-English relations in contemporary Canada, the other as the foremost historian of New France. Eccles in particular enjoyed close links with Quebec historians. Given the importance of French-English relations in the period, it seemed appropriate to build on existing strengths, and for a while that strategy bore fruit. In the late 1960s the department succeeded in hiring one of the brighter young Quebec historians, Jean-Pierre Wallot, an early nineteenth-century specialist, and in the early 1970s it tried to hire a twentieth-century counterpart. But it failed, and soon after Wallot also departed. Cook had already resigned, in 1968, and Eccles eventually retired. Although the department maintained positions in Quebec history, its newer appointments in that field, Arthur Silver and

Allan Greer, were both, obviously, not French Canadians by origin.

The Department of History during the 1970s and 1980s was able to entice faculty from other venues. The University of Alberta contributed two, Dalhousie one, Calgary one, Maine one, and Vanderbilt one. There were a variety of motives that might have affected the decision to come to Toronto, but the desire to take a pay cut was presumably not among them.

The average age and qualifications of new arrivals rose substantially during the 1970s and 1980s. The late 1960s witnessed a number of appointments that were, as the phrase went, ABDS (All But Dissertations). They were expected to finish up as best they could in evenings and summers; and they usually did. Two who did not were gently let go in the mid-1970s. By then, an ABD was almost unthinkable: completed PhDs with evidence of publishing potential were the least that would be expected.

There was little controversy over the basic qualifications to demand from potential appointees to the history department. There was rather more when it came to the subjects they were expected to teach. The department in the 1960s had divided into a number of "areas" – British, medieval, American, Canadian, European, and "other," which included Asian, African, and Latin American. To these was added International Relations – what would once have been described as diplomatic history but which, by the 1980s, had taken on a revivified identity as a key subject during the unexpected dénouement of the Cold War. The areas worked more or less well (some more, some less) in recommending and then competing for hiring priorities to the department as a whole. Certain areas recreated, within a narrower compass, the intimacy and sociability that had once existed for the department as a whole, before the ballooning effect of the 1960s made it impossible to assemble the whole department and its spouses in anything but a very large room.

The controversy among the areas arose because of the relative scarcity of new "hires." The scarcity of appointments in turn derived from the scarcity of money, as the federal government and its provincial counterpart cut back on the funds allocated to higher education. Each turn of the fiscal screw stimulated a contraction in the structures and practices of the University of Toronto and in the expectations of the history department.

In a certain sense, the university was returning to normal after the freebooting era of the expansive 1960s. Then, professors could be (and were, in at least one case) hired sight unseen. But in earlier decades, new faculty had to be negotiated with the president or at least the dean of arts, who kept a close eye on the budget. That practice, never abandoned in form, was steadily reinforced during the 1970s. The dean of arts and science doled out "hunting licences" for hiring more and more sparingly. Eventually, even the dean's authority was undermined by the sense of fiscal panic that afflicted the university as university grants, one year after another, came in under the rate of inflation.

The university, which after all was an intellectual organization, responded by planning. Planning involved announcing future crises, stressing the importance of rational responses, and then assembling wish lists from departments. The departments, operating under the threat of cutbacks for the improvident or untruthful, were exhorted to be ruthless and realistic. Perhaps some were; certainly a great deal of history's time was spent worrying and planning. In the event, history probably did not do so badly in the only currency that counted: permanent replacements for permanent losses through retirements.

In an earlier and simpler time, discussing policy or practice with the central administration was a matter of telephoning the president or his executive assistant. Chairmen, it was understood, could do that: it was one reason why they (and they alone, in the 1950s and early 1960s) had phones in their offices. In the 1970s it was still possible for chairs to phone the dean; but by the 1980s even the dean's ability to make large, untrammelled decisions was in question.

This posed something of a dilemma to chairmen (a term that was falling out of use by the 1970s and 1980s). There were five of these in our period; the sixth, an acting chair, was appointed just as this book was going to press. Archie (A.P.) Thornton, a historian of the British Empire, became chair in 1967, and so presided over the disappearance of the honours course and the inauguration of the university's New Programme.

In terms of departmental politics, Thornton was seen as a compromise candidate between Bill Nelson and Jim Conacher. The difference between these two men is not easily described. In age, training, and appearance they were relatively close. In terms of the department's history, Conacher was an insider and Nelson a perennial outsider – on the political rather than the personal side. Their rivalry drew upon style and attitude as well as substantial differences over policy. It would be going too far to say that the department divided into clear factions, and the differences that existed can easily be exaggerated. Compared with other situations in other departments, the Department of History conserved a unity of purpose with an absence of public quarrels.

The rivalry between Conacher and Nelson was more directly expressed in 1972, when the two competed directly for the chair. This time there was no compromise candidate, and Conacher prevailed. Conacher was succeeded in 1977 by Bill Callahan, a specialist in Spanish history and the first American-born chairman of the department; Callahan in turn gave way to Paul Rutherford, a Canadianist and the department's youngest chairman. Callahan, Rutherford, and Rutherford's replacement, Michael Finlayson, signalled the gradual passing of the older generation that had come out of the war. By 1990 the veterans of the Second World War were entirely gone, replaced by baby boomers who were themselves starting to grey at the temple and fray at the waistline.

Chairs were appointed with what may be termed the support or consensus of the department. Formal elections were not held, but the effect of the polling and opinion-seeking that was carried on was much the same. Those with the most backing among faculty members prevailed, though the appointment still, strictly speaking, was the dean's.

The department, like other parts of the university, was buffeted by the winds of fashion. It had first to adapt to the disappearance through combination of the honours /general distinction. Courses after 1970 referred only to individual units of instruction; those taking such courses could have come from either the general or the honours stream. The department was initially curious as to what had happened, and happily reported in 1971 that as far as could be seen the effect of the merger was to raise, not lower, grades when the contrary might have been expected. The average in history department courses, the academic secretary recorded, had shifted upward by 5 per cent. "It is difficult," he said, "to escape the conclusion that either the quality of student work has improved rather suddenly, or the department's marks have been somewhat inflated."[3]

Grading apart, and the evidence there is spare though interesting, lectures and lecture courses did not change much during the 1970s. That fact is itself remarkable. The New Programme was built on existing courses; faculty were not required or expected to alter what they taught, though in a few cases "interdisciplinary" offerings caught the imagination and were cited with high approval by the proponents of the new curriculum.[4] The New Programme simply removed the superstructure that once contained the courses and left the courses to float for themselves in a sea of students. Short of retirement, dismissal, or death, there was thereafter almost no way to sink a course as long as its faculty captain chose to keep it going.

The department taught a series of "core courses," with a 200 prefix – the second-year courses that had been the foundation of the old honours course. Canadian history enjoyed a particular popularity in a nationalist decade. Less popular, over time, were the first-year or 100-level courses that were intended to introduce undergraduates to the study of history. The old History 1b, the department's equivalent of Western Civilization, was abolished, and students were set what the department believed to be more challenging and more relevant courses. The number varied. In 1981-2, for example, students could choose among "The Emergence of the Third World," "Historians through Time," "Ideology and Society in Western Civilization," and "Legend, Myth and History." These courses certainly attracted their followers, but, under the New Programme, nobody had to take them. Enrolment therefore never quite matched what it had been under the old honours and pass courses. Instead, students were seen to be proceeding directly to area studies, the 200-series courses: Canada, Russia, or the United States, to name only a few.

One of the characteristics of the period was the ballooning of the curriculum. More courses were offered in a wider variety of subjects than ever before. In 1981-2 sixty-seven faculty offered a grand total of 135 courses: four in the 100 series, twenty in the 200 series, sixty-four on the 300 level, and forty-seven on the 400 level. The bulk of the 300 series were lecture courses, often on quite specialized topics; the 400 series were entirely seminars, the direct descendants of the old special subjects so highly prized and sought after by senior staff back in the 1940s and 1950s.

History thus combined elements of its tradition – the fourth-year seminars and the second-year survey courses – with certain novelties. Professors could not only offer seminars but they could actually lecture in their areas of specialty. The results may well have been a more varied curriculum than was offered anywhere else, and it was a significant benefit to be able to teach one's area of specialization. Even the undergraduates had the term "specialists" slapped on them in return for achieving an approved degree of concentration of studies.

Admittedly, the term was university-wide and not confined to the Department of History.

Professors could do this because their time was largely though not entirely released from tutorials. Courses in the 200-series were generally team-taught, so that teaching on that level could easily be combined with a 300-series course and a 400-series or graduate-level seminar (the latter being numbered in the 1000s). Tutorials became largely the province of graduate teaching assistants, TAS, who in some courses handled virtually all contact with students, including the grading of final exams. This practice differentiated history from certain other departments such as political economy, where final exams remained strictly the responsibility of faculty.

Some of the time saved in tutorials was ploughed back into work on committees and in meetings. The department's committee structure changed several times during this period, and the intricacies of the changes need not concern us. For most of the period under consideration the central committee was Appointments, Promotions and Tenure, or AP and T. There were eleven other committees, from budget to a "house committee" that attempted to keep an eye on the department's limited amenities. There were, as well, the areas, which in 1975 were American, Canadian, British, European, Eastern European, Third World, Medieval, and Colonial. Faculty could be, and were, members of more than one area. Inside the areas, topics such as social history (including labour history – though labour history at Toronto and elsewhere recalled the forms of political history, transferred to a more restricted scale) were more likely to occur than in the past. To these would be added new subjects, especially women's studies, which, with Sylvia Van Kirk, became a strong part of the university curriculum in the 1980s. Robert Harvey applied multidisciplinary skills to the study of multiculturalism.

These new subjects were not always welcome or understood. The story, apparently true, is still told that when Ned Shorter's *History of*

Women's Bodies was published, one senior historian staunchly refused to concede that it could possibly be history, despite the international notice and frequent acclaim it received.

With women's studies came a new emphasis on hiring women. Women, while never entirely absent from the faculty roster, were nevertheless in a tiny minority even in the 1970s. Vi Colman (appointed 1965), Ann Robson (appointed 1967), and Jill Conway (appointed 1964) were the sum total. Understandably, pressure increased on the department to appoint more: Claire LaVigna in 1970, Sylvia Van Kirk in 1975, Laurel MacDowall in 1981, Lynne Viola in 1988, among others – bearing in mind the fewer permanent appointments being made.

These figures to some degree understate the numbers in the department. There were in fact two departments of history in the 1970s and 1980s: undergraduate and graduate. The undergraduate department included the St George campus and Erindale; the graduate department counted Scarborough as well. Scarborough effectively maintained its independence on the undergraduate level while drawing on the main department for graduate teaching assistanrts and allowing its faculty to participate in the main department's graduate program.

The department's central administration became more complex. Administration co-opted faculty members, but it also employed a growing number of purely administrative staff. There was no longer a departmental secretary, but a business officer managing budgets and negotiating, on and off between November and June, the department's accounts. As money grew tighter, so did the dean of arts and science's attempts to control departmental budgeting. The department's interest, naturally, was to retain as much fiscal autonomy as it possibly could, and the result might be described as a form of creative tension.[5]

Salaries and budgets were no longer as simple as they once had been. For one thing, the professoriate was unpredictable in its movements:

a leave here, a visiting lectureship there, a fellowship somewhere else, and the department could be faced with last-minute replacements. Given the tendency of high-salaried professors to receive grants and take leave, that usually meant that last-minute money became available. Of that, the dean seized some and the department spent whatever it could salvage from the total, whether on teaching assistants or on new junior faculty: very junior, usually, with pay to match. As in any large hierarchy, such matters were very specific and were handled by specialists.

There had been, since the 1960s, an associate chairman, an undergraduate secretary, and a graduate secretary. The associate handled matters administrative and conferred with the chairman whenever the latter felt uneasy, which, in a sign of the times, was often enough. The chairman and associate occupied the two east-end offices on the second floor of Sidney Smith Hall; between them and around them was an administrative and secretarial staff that sorted out the details of undergraduate and graduate life.

Down the hall was an office reserved to the History Students' Union, a creation of the late 1960s. The HSU supervised and published course evaluations for the history department – a student's vade-mecum that assisted in identifying courses good and bad in ways that George Wrong would have found alarming. (One course was described, in the terms of the day, as an opportunity for the professor "to rap with his commie friends." More often criticism was further to the left, but on the whole it was both fair-minded and rather mild.) But the course evaluations, unthinkable in a more hierarchical time, were accepted with barely a peep.

Students, both undergraduate and graduate, elected and sent representatives to department meetings. They were a minority there and remained so, despite periodic agitation elsewhere in the faculty for "parity" – that is, equal student representation. No students sat on the AP and T committee, and hiring policy continued to be the exclusive domain of the faculty. For the most part faculty-student relationships, inside and outside the HSU, were cordial and co-operative. In this the history department was not unusual, although some other departments certainly fared worse.

Student power waxed and then waned. If the early and mid 1970s were a period of assertiveness, the later 1970s and 1980s were far less so, leaving faculty to wonder, occasionally, when or if the cycle would come round again.

Cycles of a different sort prevailed on the academic side of the department's business. Again, history was a participant at a larger university-wide feast, as the New Programme was evaluated, re-evaluated, praised, and scorned. In a free market, which the New Programme permitted and even encouraged, everyone was supposed to be able to make a rational choice. But could they? Ann Robson, Bertie Wilkinson's daughter, was especially scornful. "Is everybody happy?" she asked. Perhaps, in the short term, everybody was, but that was to take a very superficial view of a student's real needs. "What is making a student happy is not necessarily what ought to make a student happy," she continued. "[The] faculty are better able than the student to determine the contents of a university program; the latter is in most cases unable to see beyond his present needs and interests."[6]

Robson argued that the needs of the discipline were as important as the needs of the student, and should never be sacrificed for expediency or short-term satisfaction. It was a point of view that was probably in the minority when she wrote, in 1972, but over time it acquired more support. Eventually structure and sequence tended to reappear, as "specialist" degrees were reinforced and "majors" pumped up. By 1990 the term "honours" was even coming into vogue again, though with a different content from what it had meant twenty-five years before.

The balance betwen innovation and tradition remains in doubt. If reformers have become less enthusiastic over time, those who favour the nostalgia principle have not escaped many of the effects of the New Programme. Yet those effects are not what they are often thought to be. Structure and sequence as principles in the education of historians continue to command support, but, since the New Programme, structure and sequence have had to make do with course offerings that are extremely varied and highly individualistic.

These offerings also reflect the publishing activities of the faculty. Toronto was always a "publishing" department, but in the 1970s it seems to have become more so. A very crude calculation indicates an odd ratio: before 1970 those who left the department were likely to publish more than those who stayed; after 1970 the situation is reversed. Those who left tended to publish less than those who stayed.[7] There is no doubt that department members had more opportunity after 1970 than before to pursue their individual interests, and that those interests were at least partly expressed in books.

The liberalism that triumphed with the New Programme and the wide-open curriculum was not so much collective as individual, and it is difficult to contemplate how, in the future, individual rights and collective interest will ever quite combine again. At the same time, individualism in scholarship has meant that a greater and more imaginative variety of history can be and is offered to students than ever before, and that the linkage between scholarship and teaching is more firmly made than in the past. A specialized teacher has no need to scramble to keep half a lecture ahead of the class; and, as Bill Nelson predicted in 1966, many of the students in such a class will take it because they want to, not because of a rigid course prescription. The balance is evenly drawn.

In one other respect the Department of History has changed very considerably since the 1960s. Before 1970 history's geography was uncomplicated. Physically and spiritually the department lived and worked together. The department lived in Sidney Smith Hall, scattered over three floors, but focused on a common front office and centred on a single line of authority, from dean to chairman to department.

When not on leave, historians used their offices for their work. Though teatime no longer existed as a social link, there was a coffee shop in off-hours and the Faculty Club at lunch. Historians at the suburban campuses had different points of focus, which differentiated them somewhat from their downtown colleagues, but they also had the advantage of being a smaller and therefore more cohesive group.

Sidney Smith Hall had its drawbacks, but they did not prevent the department from functioning more or less as it always had until the mid 1970s. At about that time a combination of factors began to predominate (they had always existed to some extent) that worked to loosen ties among historians – as among other academic professionals. And at that point Sidney Smith's lack of attractiveness began to count, strongly and negatively, in the department's daily life.

The first influence was the appearance of alternatives. Better offices than Sidney Smith's existed around the university, but they were mostly in the colleges. The colleges reserved their offices for their own faculties who, with very few exceptions, taught the "old college subjects" from English to ethics. The trouble with the colleges, those that were "federated" rather than directly owned by the university, was that they were traditionally impoverished and then untraditionally broke. The university rescued them through a "memorandum of understanding" that effectively nationalized their teaching staffs except for theology. The college subjects became university subjects, and the colleges' preoccupation with them diminished to the point where the link between "college subject" and "college office" was snapped.

College offices now became available. Colleges lost little time in asking various members of formerly "university" departments, like history, to associate themselves, in return for a little fellowship and a lot of time. Beginning in the early 1970s, historians began to migrate. The flow included a former chairman, Archie Thornton, Bill Nelson, and Craig Brown, a former associate chairman, to University College. Others, including the author, ended up at Trinity, which encouraged foreign policy specialists to join its newly founded interdisciplinary program in international relations.

Other historians found that in the age of the computer they were no longer as tied to a central office as they once had been. Increasingly the front office existed to administer programs and service students, and not to handle the secretarial chores of department members. Sabbatical leaves and leave fellowships, once confined to a very few, became commonplace, while the diversity of research interests among faculty meant that in research years or seasons the faculty were scattered in distant lands, no longer clustered around the National Archives in Ottawa or the Public Record Office in London. If geography had become disjointed, so had time.

And so had the discipline. Historians in Wrong's day, and in Chester Martin's, enjoyed the comfortable feeling of belonging to a single, discrete discipline. There was an assumption that historians could and should know the various fields within history, and that no field was so complicated that it could not be converted, as required, into lectures for undergraduates. The expectation, as a general rule, was that a student could read a text or follow a lecture, but that an adequate performance would not demand both.

Professionalism and specialization transformed the system of knowledge that historians were expected to master. Instead of two or three books on eighteenth-century Germany, there were scores and then hundreds, all published by respectable university or other scholarly presses. Where once the *Canadian Historical Review* ruled the roost, there were five and then ten competing journals. And where once the University of Toronto was unquestionably pre-eminent among Canadian universities, it found its standing diminished as rivals created their own centres of specialized scholarship.

In a world of specialization, the historians at the University of

Toronto performed well. In a world of rivalries, the university found it could compete, and that its historians could match in quality or quantity what was being produced elsewhere – certainly in Canada but to a very large extent in the United States as well. Medieval history in particular was pre-eminent, but other fields, such as Canadian or British, also prevailed. Though the university did well by contemporary standards, it also suffered from the deficits that characterized the historical profession elsewhere in the late twentieth century.

History as George Wrong and his successors conceived it was an integrative discipline. In practice at the University of Toronto the study of history, either from a learning or a teaching point of view, was a subject that could be, and was, "swotted up" for lectures or exams. In brief, it was the world where Lester Pearson could read his students the latest play about Oliver Cromwell in lieu of a lecture, and thereby cover off a couple of seventeenth-century decades. The kind of history studied in the 1920s and 1930s was accessible to all, or almost all, though more as a lesson in public speaking or in civic duty than as scholarly history.

In the 1920s and 1930s, colleagues read one another's books and travelled to summer or winter conventions where all the academic historians in the country could assemble in one room or, if it were the United States, in a hotel ballroom or a large gym. The younger historians hired at the end of the 1920s, people like Donald Creighton, helped change that; and the historians of the next generation, educated at Toronto in the 1930s and hired there in the 1940s or 1950s, changed it still more. They stretched the prevailing system as far as it could go, to the point recognized in the 1962 curricular reforms.

Their views and practices were recognizable to their successors in the 1970s, but by that point the intellectual universe had changed almost out of recognition. It was still possible for a historian to study a variety of fields, or to leave behind safe national turf for a larger domain. But to do it he or she would have to become an expert in that other field, to re-professionalize in another direction.[8] Such people were not uncommon at Toronto in the 1980s or 1990s: John Beattie, Michael Bliss, Michael Marrus, Ned Shorter, and Paul Rutherford come to mind as examples of intellectual transference.

The computer revolution of the 1970s, at first mystifying and then universal, turned some of the best minds of a generation to a world of statistics and models and directed funding into new and very expensive channels. The results were fascinating to some and frustrating to others; the effect, in terms of the universal comprehension of history, was more divisive than not.

Interdisciplinary travel therefore did not mean that the fragmentation characteristic of twentieth-century historical specialization was diminished. While some historians reached out to the social scientists via "cliometrics," quantitative history, others reconfirmed their identity as humanists. Inside the university, history, once generally regarded as a social science closely akin to political science or sociology, was officially classed as a "humanity."

The precise definition, the exact place, of history in the intellectual world of the 1990s is not a point on which most historians can agree. That at least is reminiscent of the historians of the past, who eschewed theory, for the most part, in favour of practicality. Historians have concentrated on what they do, and left the theorizing to others. Oddly, for a group so concerned with the past, they have generally said and done little about their own. They act as the past's interpreters, and not as its subject.

In examining the record of the University of Toronto's Department of History there are obvious consistencies. History as studied at Toronto is and has been a part of a greater whole. Daniel Wilson, when he came to Toronto to be its first historian (and anthropologist and English professor) brought, as he was expected to do, a part of a larger culture.

The purpose of his work was to communicate a sense of the past to Canadians, and in doing so Wilson was one of the first to integrate Canada's more recent past into "history." Wilson did more than bring an academic subject to Upper Canada: he also began to create a unique educational system on which his successor, George Wrong, built the particular tutorial structure of the history department of the University of Toronto.

That system, much changed and sometimes battered, has endured. Tutorials still exist, though alongside a greatly expanded department with one of the most varied curricula of any university in Canada or North America. The variety, an indirect product of the expansion of the university in the 1960s, marks a second foundation for the department: a modification of its nature to satisfy the capacities of its staff while offering an unusual range of intellectual experience to its students. The liberalism of the late nineteenth century – the pursuit of excellence through merit and the encouragement of merit through attention to teaching in small groups – thus combines with the liberalism of the twentieth century in the communication of the variety of human experience and the provision of freedom of choice.

This liberalism is a fitting epitaph for a institution that exists for the purpose of liberal education. In this the department, and the university of which it is a part, are true to the society that created them.

Notes

CHAPTER 1 BY WAY OF PROLOGUE

1 J.M.S. Careless, "Robert Baldwin," in Careless, ed., The Pre-Confederation Premiers: Ontario Government Leaders, 1841-1867 (Toronto 1980), 134
2 W.G. Ormsby, "Sir Francis Hincks," ibid., 175
3 Carl Berger, "Sir Daniel Wilson," Dictionary of Canadian Biography, XII (Toronto 1990), 1109-14
4 John Higham, History: The Development of Historical Studies in the United States (Princeton 1965), 4
5 Robin Harris, English Studies at Toronto: A History (Toronto 1988), 12
6 University of Toronto Archives (UTA), Senate minutes, Acc. A70-00051001
7 The Globe, 7 December 1852. I am indebted to Alex Reford for this reference.

8 J.W. Burrow, A Liberal Descent: Victorian Historians and the English Past (Cambridge 1983), 98
9 Peter Novick, That Noble Dream: The "Objectivity Question" and the American Historical Profession (New York 1988), 21-31, notes that Ranke was more often misinterpreted than truly understood; that this pre-eminently scientific symbol also stood for a romantic, "psychedelic" mode of understanding history.
10 A.B. McKillop, A Disciplined Intelligence (Toronto 1979), 30; Wilson quoted in Claude Bissell, University College: A Portrait (Toronto 1953), 39
11 UTA, Daniel Wilson Papers, B45-0014, box 004, 22 September 1853
12 W.S. Wallace, A History of the University of Toronto 1827-1927 (Toronto 1927), 122; Hector Charlesworth, More Candid

Chronicles (Toronto 1928), 50

13 Wilson diary, November 1853, passim

14 Charlesworth, More Candid Chronicles, 49

15 Bruce Hodgins, "John Sandfield Macdonald," in Careless, ed., Pre-Confederation Premiers, 298

16 Berger, "Wilson," 1112

17 W.I. Alexander, The University of Toronto and Its Colleges 1827-1906 (Toronto 1906), 84-5

18 See I.M. Drummond, Political Economy at the University of Toronto: A History of the Department, 1885-1982 (Toronto 1983), 6, 23.

19 Ibid., 37

20 By the twentieth century, honours courses included "pass options," courses that were intended to broaden the otherwise excessively specialized nature of the honours courses and that required only a passing grade. These "pass courses" must be distinguished from the pass course: all of which makes it far less perplexing to use the term "general course" from now on.

21 William Duncan Meikle, "And Gladly Teach: G.M. Wrong and the Department of History of the University of Toronto" (PhD thesis, Michigan State University 1977), 8

22 The same was true of English. See Harris, English Studies at Toronto, 14.

23 Burton J. Bledstein, The Culture of Professionalism: The Middle Class and the Rise of Higher Education in America (New York 1976), 279-80

24 UTA, Fran Dale Papers, notes of conversation with Professor G.H. Needler, 16 November 1957. Needler was born in 1866, and graduated from the university in 1886.

25 The Globe, 9 February 1890, letter from Professor William Dale

26 University calendars, 1885-9

27 Wilson diary, 1 January 1881

28 In fairness, it should be noted that Wilson did not consider himself a foe of women's education; he would have preferred women's colleges along the lines of Vassar in the United States. Berger, "Wilson," 1113

29 Wilson diary, 30 May 1880, 28 October and 1 November 1882

30 Ibid., 2 and 5 June, 11 September 1888

31 Ibid., 7 June 1891

32 Ibid., 15 February 1890, 9 March 1891

CHAPTER 2 SALAD DAYS

1 UTA, Fran Dale Papers, W.S. Wallace to Dale, 3 September 1957
2 Ontario Archives, Education Department Records, Letters to the Minister 1880-1905, Blake to George Ross, 27 July 1892
3 The Globe, 2 February 1895, letter from B.E. Walker
4 Alan Bowker, "Truly Useful Men: Maurice Hutton, George Wrong, James Mavor and the University of Toronto, 1880-1927" (PhD thesis, University of Toronto 1975), 300n
5 UTA, George Wrong Papers, 1892 diary, 26 July 1892, 248
6 Ibid., nd, 4
7 Bowker, "Truly Useful Men," 72-6
8 Ibid., 2-6
9 See, for example, Sir Daniel Wilson's letter of 26 September 1890 to A.S. Hardy, provincial secretary, on "The Recent Appointments" to the university; it was reprinted in The Globe on 30 September.
10 Wrong adored Sir Wilfrid Laurier and supported him through every election except 1917. In 1911 he even offered to campaign for

Laurier and reciprocity. Bowker, "Truly Useful Men," 91
11 UTA, Falconer Papers, Mavor to Falconer, nd [May 1910]
12 University Calendar, 1892-3
13 Hector Charlesworth, More Candid Chronicles (Toronto 1928), 65; The Globe, 9 February 1895, letter from Professor William Dale
14 Varsity, 17 October 1894, editorial, "A Recent Appointment"
15 See note 13.
16 University Calendar, 1892-3, 109-10
17 Bowker, "Truly Useful Men," 24
18 Quoted ibid., 9
19 Ibid., 10-11
20 Quoted ibid., 123
21 Ian Drummond, Political Economy at the University of Toronto: A History of the Department (Toronto 1983), 34-6
22 Bowker, "Truly Useful Men," 124-5; Drummond, Political Economy, 29
23 Charlesworth, More Candid Chronicles, 72-3
24 Ibid., 65-6
25 Dale Papers, Dale letter, 5 February 1895
26 Ibid., Joseph Montgomery to Fran Dale, 5 August 1957; W.S. Wallace to Fran Dale, 3

September 1957, contended that Mulock had forced the issue so as to replace Blake as chancellor.

27 Ibid., Fran Dale's notes of conversation with Professor William Needler, who had shared digs with William Dale in 1894.

28 Varsity, 17, 31 October, 7, 14 November 1894

29 The Globe, 4 February 1894. Walker was one of Toronto's most prominent citizens, a patron of the arts, and later a member of the university's Board of Governors, which he supervised from his home "Long Garth" at 99 St George Street. On Wrong, see Bowker, "Truly Useful Men," 341.

30 Charlesworth, More Candid Chronicles, 76-8

31 Roger Graham, Arthur Meighen, I (Toronto 1960), 22-3

32 Report of the Commission on Discipline and Other Matters in the University of Toronto (Toronto 1895), 11-12

33 UTA, Presidential Records: Robert Falconer, Mavor to Falconer, nd [May 1910]

34 Drummond, Political Economy, 36-7

35 Bowker, "Truly Useful Men," 245

36 Ibid., 105

37 He moved into the Jarvis Street house after Blake left for England in 1892: Bowker, "Truly Useful Men," 77.

38 Quoted ibid., 92

39 Quoted ibid., 223. Wrong was criticizing the appointment of a rich businessman, Peter Larkin, to be high commissioner to Great Britain, a post that Wrong considered was not unsuited to his own talents.

40 Ibid., 224

41 Ibid., 214

42 Quoted ibid., 106

43 Paul Martin interview, 6 April 1991

44 On Wrong's anti-politics see Bowker, "Truly Useful Men," 260

45 Paul Phillips, Britain's Past in Canada: The Teaching and Writing of British History (Vancouver 1989), 39-40

46 Wrong, quoted ibid., 35

47 Alexander, a native of Hamilton and a Toronto graduate, was himself something of a professional prodigy, having taken a degree in classics from the University of London and then recycled himself with a PhD in English from Johns Hopkins. English and History

constituted a "graduating department," and as such met regularly until the course was "withdrawn" in 1937. Robin Harris, *English Studies at Toronto* (Toronto 1988), 49-50

48 University Calendar, 1904-5, 128-9, 157-8

49 Ibid., 1905-6, 166-7

50 Falconer Papers, Mavor to Falconer, nd [May 1910]

51 Ibid.

52 R. Hodder Williams, "The Tutorial Experiment," *University Monthly*, February 1915, 196

53 Letter of 1902, quoted in W.D. Meikle, "And Gladly Teach: G.M. Wrong and the Department of History at the University of Toronto" (PhD thesis, Michigan State University 1977), 119

54 R. Douglas Francis, *Frank H. Underhill: Intellectual Provocateur* (Toronto 1986), 15

55 Hodder Williams, "Tutorial Experiment," 198

56 Meikle, "And Gladly Teach," 105

57 On Kenney's background see Glenn T. Wright, "James F. Kenney: Pioneer Irish Scholar," Canadian Catholic Historical Association, *Study Sessions*, 19, 651-2

58 NA, J.L. Kenney Papers, vol. 7, Kenney diary, 8 October

1904. Kenney's diary is less a daily chronicle than a monthly memoir.

59 Ibid., 4 June 1906

60 Meikle, "And Gladly Teach," 94-6

61 Kenney diary, 30 October 1904

62 Bowker, "Truly Useful Men," 308

63 Kenney diary, 21 January 1907

64 Bowker, "Truly Useful Men," 303

65 Charles Humphries, *"Honest Enough to Be Bold": The Life and Times of Sir James Pliny Whitney* (Toronto 1985), 108-9

66 Ibid., 126-8

67 Drummond, *Political Economy*, 45-6

68 Bowker, "Truly Useful Men," 301-2

69 Letter of 15 May 1925, quoted in Meikle, "And Gladly Teach," 107

70 Quoted ibid., 91

71 See Michael Bliss, *A Canadian Millionaire: The Life and Business Times of Sir Joseph Flavelle, Bart.* (Toronto 1978), 203; and Bowker, "Truly Useful Men," 307 n67.

72 Quoted in Meikle, "And Gladly Teach," 109

73 Claude Bissell, *The Young Vincent Massey* (Toronto 1981), 38.

Bissell terms Wrong's basic argument as one of "superior inequality." Wrong argued on sociological grounds that women and men were called to different roles in society and that their education ought to reflect that difference.

74 Letter of 2 October 1915, quoted in Meikle, "And Gladly Teach," 108

75 Ibid., 98n

76 Bowker, "Truly Useful Men," 307

77 President's Reports, 1902-8

78 University Calendar, 1913-14, 162-4

79 Falconer Papers, Mavor to Falconer [May 1910]

80 Gary Kelly, *Historical Club of the University of Toronto: List of Members and Subjects for the Years 1905 to 1960* (Toronto 1964)

81 Kenney diary, 4 June 1906

82 Ibid., 21 January 1907

83 Ibid., 4 June 1906

84 Francis, *Underhill*, 18-19

85 NA, Frank Underhill Papers, vol. 90, have an extensive set of club programs.

86 Francis, *Underhill*, 19

87 It is a better indicator than, for example, the Royal Society of Canada, which John Porter used as a sign of elite status in his *Vertical Mosaic: A Analysis of Social Class and Power in Canada* (Toronto 1965).

88 There are some interesting indications in Chad Gaffield, Lynne Marks, and Susan Laskin, "Student Populations and Graduate Careers: Queen's University, 1895-1900," in P. Axelrod and J.G. Reid, eds., *Youth, University and Canadian Society* (Toronto 1989), 3-21. Some of the argument in Burton J. Bledstein, *The Culture of Professionalism: The Middle Class and the Development of Higher Education in America* (New York 1976), may apply, particularly the assertion that turn-of-the-century universities were client-oriented institutions (299).

89 Brian McKillop, "Marching as to War: Elements of Ontario Undergraduate Culture, 1880-1914," in Axelrod and Reid, eds., *Youth*, 79-80

90 Bledstein, *Culture of Professionalism*, 288

91 John English, *Shadow of Heaven: The Life of Lester Pearson*, I (Toronto 1989), 26

92 Kylie's parents were paid his full salary until 30 June 1916 by the Board of Governors: President's Report, 1916.

93 President's Report, 1914, 1915, 1916, 1917, 1918, 1919. Honours history enrolments in 1914-15 were

204; in 1915-16, 212; in 1916-17, 126; in 1917-18, 148; and in 1918-19, 200.

94 Meikle, "And Gladly Teach," 108

95 Drummond, *Political Economy*, 36-7

96 Quoted in Douglas Owram, *The Government Generation: Canadian Intellectuals and the State* (Toronto 1986), 80

97 Quoted in Phillips, *Britain's Past in Canada*, 57

98 English, *Shadow of Heaven*, 58

99 UTA, University Historian's Records, A83-0036/006, Wrong to Falconer, 22 May 1922

100 Paul Martin interview, 6 April 1991. Martin, who was not a member, recalls being invited once by the father, once by the son, and once by himself.

101 An Englishman, Flenley had taken his BA at Liverpool and then a B.Litt. at Oxford in 1910.

CHAPTER 3 A NATIONAL INSTITUTION

1 University of Toronto Archives (UTA), University Historian's Records, box 6, Wrong to Falconer, 19 May and 9 June 1923

2 Ibid., box 6, Wrong to Falconer, 19 May 1923

3 David O. Levine, *The American College and the Culture of Aspiration* (Ithaca 1986), 96. Levine notes the popularity of courses based on Oxford's "Greats," which impressed American Rhodes Scholars.

4 University Historian's Records, box 6, Wrong to Falconer, 17 April 1923

5 Ibid., box 6, Falconer to A.B. Corey, 1924

6 UTA, A73-0026/075(29), File Cumberland, Frederick William, MP

7 Urwick to Falconer, 29 November 1929, quoted in Ian Drummond, *Political Economy at the University of Toronto* (Toronto 1983), 59

8 UTA, History Department Records, box 5, Wrong to Colonel LePan, 1 October 1924

9 Richard Saunders interview, January 1991

10 History Department Records, box 4, Wrong to Mabel M. Martin, St Hilda's College, 6 May 1926

11 Saunders interview, January 1991

12 John Cairns to author, nd [June 1991]

13 University Historian's Records, box 6, J.J. Talman to Robin Harris, 23 March 1973

14 History Department Records,

general correspondence, Martin to J.D. Keans, 12 October 1934, quoted in W.D. Meikle, "And Gladly Teach: G.M. Wrong and the Department of History at the University of Toronto" (PhD thesis, Michigan State University 1977), 223

15 Ibid., 224

16 Ibid.

17 Charles P. Stacey, *A Date with History: Memoirs of a Canadian Historian* (Ottawa 1983), 14

18 Ibid., 15

19 Ibid.; Ken McNaught interview, 14 January 1991; University Historian's Records, box 6, Brebner to Falconer, 12 February 1929

20 History Department Records, box 6, Wallace to George Wrong, 17 October 1926

21 There is a contrast between Canadian and American experiences in the 1920s. In the United States the total number of undergraduate students grew considerably in that decade; in both Canada and Ontario the growth was by approximately 20 per cent, in Canada's case to not quite 33,000 in 1930 (graduate and undergraduate combined): *Historical Statistics of Canada*, 2nd ed., (Ottawa 1983), W340-8, W394-402. The comparable figure for the United States is 1.1 million: Levine, *American College*, 38-9.

22 University Historian's Records, Hume Wrong to Falconer, 9 February 1927

23 Ibid., G.M Smith to Falconer, 1 March 1927

24 Ibid., A83-0036/006, G.M. Smith to Falconer, 1 March 1927

25 John English, *Shadow of Heaven: The Life of Lester Pearson* I (Toronto 1989), 100

26 University Historian's Records, Falconer to Wrong, 8 June 1922, in which the proposal is mentioned.

27 University Historian's Records, Falconer to Underhill, 3 May 1927

28 Ibid., Smith to Falconer, 3 May 1927

29 Ibid., Falconer to Wrong, 28 February 1919

30 Ibid., Smith to Falconer, 16 March 1927

31 Ibid., Smith to Falconer, 16 June 1927, and Falconer to Smith, 24 June 1927

32 UTA, Falconer Papers, A67-1007/110a, vol. 110a, Smith to Falconer, 3 July 1927

33 History Department Papers, General Correspondence, A70-025, box 1, [George Smith?]

to Creighton, 14 April 1927

34 University Historian's Records, box 6, McDougall to McNeil, 12 April 1928, and Falconer to McNeil, 26 May 1928

35 Ibid., Kenneth Bell to Smith, nd [Nov. 1927], enclosed in typescript in Smith to Falconer, 11 November 1927

36 English, Shadow of Heaven, 133-4

37 Ibid., 138-40

38 Falconer Papers, box 116, Smith to Falconer, 14 August 1928

39 History Department Papers, General Correspondence, Box 4, G.M. Smith to Edgar McInnis, 12 January 1926. In response to a request for recommendations, Smith asked for "the judgment of Feiling and others at Christ Church about yourself ... Be assured we shall help you to the limit of our ability."

40 History Department Records, General Correspondence, box 4, Smith to Falconer, nd [probably late August or early September 1928, misfiled under 1929]

41 Carl Berger, The Writing of Canadian History (Toronto 1986), 34-8

42 Saunders interview, January 1991

43 Cody's biography in the Canadian Who's Who for 1937-8 was twice the length of Falconer's.

44 In 1931, in second year, there were twenty-five in Modern History, of whom thirteen were women. Miss M.B. Wright got the only first. There were also twelve seconds, seven thirds, two aegrotats, and three "tr," a term that denoted compulsory transfer to the pass course. In English and History, out of forty-five students, thirty-nine were women. In Philosophy (English or History) there were ten enrolled, incuding two women.

45 All figures are from the President's Report.

46 These figures are derived from Meikle, "And Gladly Teach," appendix E.

47 Ibid., 225

48 All figures are taken from the President's Reports for the period. Miss Hahn appears on the budget for the first time in 1942-3.

49 Saunders interview, January 1991

50 Ibid.

51 University Calendar, 1928-9, 109-15

52 National Archives of Canada

(NA), Creighton Papers, vol. 24, file University of Toronto History Department 1929-38

53 University Calendar, 1932-3, 104-7

54 History Department Records, boxes 1-6, file P-Q144, R.B. Fennel to Chester Martin, 28 February 1938, asking if changing Economics 2d from compulsory to optional had the approval of the provincial Department of Education.

55 History Department Records, box 2, "The Course in Modern History," February 1930

56 Robin Harris, *English Studies at Toronto: A History* (Toronto 1988), 82-4; Vincent Bladen, *Bladen on Bladen: Memoirs of a Political Economist* (Toronto 1978), 44

57 Ontario Archives, Cody Papers, MacBrien to Cody, 6 April 1935

58 Ibid., David Walker to Cody, 8 June 1937

59 Ibid., Frank Beare to Cody, 18 April 1939

60 Quoted in Douglas Francis, *Frank H. Underhill: Intellectual Provocateur* (Toronto 1986), 111

61 Ibid., 111-13

62 Saunders interview, January 1991

63 Pickersgill to author, 15 December 1990, enclosing his essay, "The Last Challenge to the Late Frank Underhill's Position at the University of Toronto" [1987]

64 Francis, *Underhill*, 114-27

65 Sarah Campion, *Father: A Portrait of G.C. Coulton at Home* (London 1948), 175. I am indebted to T.A. Sandquist for this reference.

CHAPTER 4 AFFLUENCE

1 F.J. Thorpe to author, 20 December 1990

2 J.B. Conacher interview, 5 January 1990

3 University of Toronto Archives (UTA), George Brown Papers, vol. 24, files 14 and 15, especially Riddell to Brown, 16 October 1944, in which Riddell speculated on ways to supplement his earnings to get over "the low income period in Baldwin House."

4 Personal discussions with Charles Stacey. His situation was not unique. One economist who spent the war on leave in Ottawa was said to have been offered the same salary on his return to

Toronto in 1945 as he had on his departure in 1939. Ian Drummond, *Political Economy at the University of Toronto* (Toronto1983), 88

5 National Archives of Canada, Donald Creighton Papers, vol. 37, mark books

6 Drummond, *Political Economy*, 87-8

7 Thorpe to author, 20 December 1990

8 Ibid., 16 January 1991

9 Ibid.

10 W.H. Nelson interview, 27 May 1991

11 Confidential interview, 14 January 1991

12 Conacher interview, 5 January 1990

13 Ibid. I am grateful to ambassador Vernon Turner for lending me his undergraduate essays.

14 Thorpe to author, 16 January 1991

15 Conacher interview, 1 June 1991

16 Ibid., 5 January 1990

17 Ibid.

18 Thorpe to author, 16 January 1991

19 Ken McNaught interview

20 UTA, History Department Records, box 24, file "Appointments, '60-'61," Careless to C.H. Clough, 28 July 1961

21 Conacher interview, 5 January 1990

22 Ibid.

23 Creighton Papers, vol. 65, diary, 3 April 1953

24 Ibid., 13 March 1953

25 Creighton Papers, vol. 3, Creighton to Morton, 18 November 1957, and Morton to Creighton, 23 November 1957

26 McNaught interview, 14 January 1991

27 Ramsay Cook interview, 13 June 1991

28 Ibid.

29 W.H. Nelson interview, 27 May 1991; T.A. Sandquist interview, 29 May 1991. There are also stories of prejudice against other ethnic groups, including Jews; yet Creighton strongly supported the appointment and then the proposed return to Toronto of David Spring.

30 History Department Records, A67-0008, Dean of Arts Samuel Beatty to Sidney Smith, 8 November 1951. Beatty suggested giving the chairman only one unique power, the knowledge of all salaries in his department. Everything else, appointments, promotions, and the like, would be done by committee.

31 See the discussion in Vincent Bladen, *Bladen on Bladen: Memoirs of a Political Economist* (Toronto 1978), 126-7.

32 History Department Records, copy of Smith to McInnis, 27 February 1952, with Smith's pencilled comment

33 Creighton diary, 9 September 1952

34 Ibid., 12 March 1954

35 History Departament Records, Beatty to Smith, 10 August 1951; Martin annotation on 1951-2 budget

36 Ibid., Smith to Beatty, 4 October 1951

37 Ibid., Beatty to Smith, 19 May 1952, with comments by Smith attached

38 Ibid., A.C. Turner to Smith, 27 May 1953

39 Ibid., file "Appointments '53-54"

40 The figures were $15,000 versus $7600. Creighton diary, 21 June 1954

41 History Department Records, A67-0008, restricted budget information

42 Creighton diary, 3 December 1952, 16 and 23 January 1953. Creighton urged more efforts to attract Spring back, but failed to convince his colleagues.

43 Creighton diary, 7 June 1954

44 Bladen, *Bladen*, 126

45 R. Douglas Francis, *Frank Underhill: Intellectual Provocateur* (Toronto 1986), 160

46 Creighton Papers, vol. 3, Creighton to Frank Rogers, 14 October 1954

47 Ibid., Creighton to Dray, 29 October 1957, and Dray to Creighton, 6 November 1957

48 Margaret Banks oral history transcript, 1987, 42

49 Banks to author, 28 August 1990

50 Creighton Papers, vol. 3, Creighton to K.A. McKirdy, 16 April 1957

51 Robin Ross, *The Short Road Down: A University Changes* (Toronto 1984), 9-10

52 Underhill Papers, vol. 90, file U of T miscellaneous, Piepenburg to Underhill, nd [1954]

53 Ibid., memo Historical Club, Thursday, 27 Jan. 1955, by FHU

54 Conacher interview, 3 June 1991

55 Ramsay Cook interview, 13 June 1991

56 Robin Harris, *A History of Higher Education in Canada, 1663-1960* (Toronto 1976)

57 W.J. Eccles interview, 3 June 1991

58 Ibid.

59 Creighton Papers, vol. 37, memorandum by Gerald Craig, March 1966

60 Ibid., diary, 19 February 1962. The writing is cramped and nearly illegible.

61 Ibid., 16 March 1962

62 Creighton Papers, vol. 37, memoranda by W.H. Nelson and Gerald Craig, nd [March 1966]

63 Creighton diary, 11 April 1966

64 Ibid., diary 14 April 1966

65 R.C. Brown interview, 11 June 1991

66 Creighton diary, 16 May 1966

67 Ibid., 18 May 1966

68 History Department Records, box 003, file "Curriculum revision"

CHAPTER 5 THE FULLNESS OF TIME

1 University of Toronto Archives, History Department Records, box 20, Sandquist to Policy Committee, 26 January 1968

2 Ibid.

3 History Department Records, box 73, academic secretary to members of Standards Committee, 4 October 1971

4 Ibid., box 40, file "1969-70: Programme 1969," "Interdisciplinary Studies," nd

5 Margarita Orszag interview, 25 June 1991

6 History Department Records, box 73, Ann Robson, "One Opinion on the 'New programme,'" November 1972

7 The crudity of this calculation involves the question of defining those who left and those who stayed. G.C. Coulton's inclusion, for example, is highly doubtful, though he did write a book of memoirs while in Toronto. Then there is the question of what exactly should be included: parts of books where there is "no principal author"? pamphlets? non-historical work? Helen McMurchie Bott, after being extruded from history, became a prolific publisher in social work: presumably had she been allowed to stay in the department she would have done the same in history.

8 Paul Rutherford interview, 25 June 1991

Index